FENCES

August Wilson

AUTHORED by Lane Davis
UPDATED AND REVISED by Elizabeth Weinbloom

COVER DESIGN by Table XI Partners LLC
COVER PHOTO by Olivia Verma and © 2005 GradeSaver, LLC

BOOK DESIGN by Table XI Partners LLC

Published by GradeSaver LLC, www.gradesaver.com

First published in the United States of America by GradeSaver LLC. 2011

ISBN 978-1-60259-246-9

Printed in the United States of America

For other products and additional information please visit http://www.gradesaver.com

Table of Contents

Table of Contents

Biography of Wilson, August (1945-2005)

August Wilson was born Frederick August Kittel on April 27, 1945, in Pittsburgh, PA. His white father was not present in his childhood, and Wilson adopted his strong-willed mother's surname when he began to write. When his mother re-married, Wilson moved to a mostly white suburb, and experienced the extent of racism in the school system. After two more schools, he dropped out, and began to self-educate himself at the library.

In his twenties, Wilson decided he would be a poet, and had a few poems published in magazines. He also became familiar with and was influenced by the Black Power movement, and with some other poets he founded a theater company that served the Hill District of Pittsburgh. Still focusing primarily on his poetry, Wilson did not begin writing plays seriously until 1978, when he got a job adapting Native American folk tales into children's plays for a museum in St. Paul. Homesick for Pittsburgh, he began to write *Jitney*, which was first produced in 1982. It was quickly followed by *Ma Rainey's Black Bottom*, and the rest of Wilson's prolific output followed from there.

The next two decades were devoted to Wilson's major theatrical cycle, consisting of ten plays that chronicle the African American experience in America. Each play focuses on a different decade of the twentieth century, and all but *Ma Rainey* take place in Wilson's beloved Hill District of Pittsburgh.

Wilson's plays were quickly embraced by the theatrical mainstream - particularly the white mainstream, which caused Wilson no little distress and initiated a series of conflicts in which he insisted on the support and development of a black theater. But nearly all of his major plays were produced on Broadway (all except *Jitney*), and he received a Tony award for *Fences*, two Pulitzers for *Fences* and *The Piano Lesson*, and seven New York Drama Critics' Circle awards. His plays ran for nearly 1,800 performances on Broadway altogether, and some - particularly *Fences* - were very financially successful.

In his work, Wilson concentrated on the daily lives of average African Americans, but gave particularly poetic, lyrical voices to the lower class service workers who dominate the Hill District. His works are unique for consistently bringing out the angry, bitter stories of the poor and marginalized in a fashion that was accepted by the mainstream, while remaining politically and socially honest.

In 2005, Wilson died of liver cancer at the age of 60. The last play of his cycle, *Radio Golf*, opened at Yale Rep just months before he died, and moved to Broadway in 2007. In his honor, Broadway's Virginia Theater has been renamed the August Wilson Theater.

About Fences

Fences was written by August Wilson in 1983 and first performed at the 46th Street Theatre on Broadway in 1987. *Fences* is the sixth play in Wilson's "Pittsburgh Cycle." The Cycle is a series of plays set in Pittsburgh, Pennsylvania over the ten decades of the 20th century. *Fences* is set in the 1950's and deals with issues of race relations and the changing broader culture of the United States.

The play was both a critical and commercial success. During its initial run on Broadway, it brought in an astounding $11 million in its first year of production, a record for a non-musical play. It won four Tony Awards, including Best Play; several Critic's awards; and the Pulitzer Prize for drama. Beyond its commercial and critical success, however, Wilson's play is perhaps most notable for its impact on popular theater. *Fences*, along with Wilson's other most successful play, *Ma Rainey's Black Bottom*, proved that the theatrical tastes of the country were shifting from an appetite for popular musicals and comedies to an acceptance of serious theater dealing with the cultural, racial, and social issues of the day.

The play's impact reached beyond the theater and into the academic and artistic conversations of the late twentieth century. It has been deemed a "generational play" by critics and academics for its depiction of three generations of African-American men -- Troy Maxson, Troy's father, and Troy's son. It depicts an archetypal struggle between fathers and sons, themes that have proved pertinent across racial and generational divides. The play has even premiered in numerous foreign countries (including China), demonstrating its thematic power across cultures.

Fences is unique among Wilson's plays in that it adheres more strictly to the classical tragedy structure than his other works. Wilson often objected to such structure in his plays, yet *Fences* ultimately embraces the orderly flow of beginning, rising action, climax, and falling action. Wilson's play also features a clear protagonist, Troy Maxson, with whom the audience can identify, suffer, and become redeemed.

Though written in the 1980's, the play deals with African-American life in the post-World War II era. Troy is a product of this time, continually caught between the African-American oppression of his Southern childhood and his Northern adopted home, and his changing world - a world in which African-Americans were joining the middle class, securing better jobs, and seeing their children gain opportunities, such as college and sports careers, that previous generations never had. Troy represents an entire generation, unsatisfied with the legacy of racism that they bore and uncomfortable in their slow social ascent.

In a testament to its enduring universal themes, *Fences* was revived on Broadway in 2010, with Denzel Washington in the lead. Again, the play was nominated for multiple Tony Awards, winning Best Actor for Washington, Best Actress for Viola Davis in the part of Rose, and Best Revival. *Fences* also remains one of the most assigned theatrical texts to students in the United States, ensuring that it will continue to be the subject of academic debate for generations to come.

Character List

Troy Maxson

Troy is the protagonist of *Fences*. He is a working class African American man who lives with his wife, Rose, and son, Corey, in the Hill District of Pittsburgh. He works for the Sanitation Department as a garbage collector. Troy is a tragic-hero; he is dedicated to a fault to providing for his family and to making sure his sons have better lives than he has had. He was once a great baseball player in the Negro Leagues, but he was too old to join the Major Leagues when they were integrated. His past mistakes and failures greatly influence his outlook on life and his relationship with his sons.

Rose Maxson

Rose is Troy's second wife, who he married after being released from prison. Troy maintains an affectionate patriarchal relationship with Rose, demanding respect from her as the head of the household and primary bread winner, though he is greatly influenced by her realistic take on the changing world. Rose is the mother of Corey, Troy's youngest son.

Gabriel Maxson

Gabriel, or Gabe, is Troy's brother. He suffered a traumatic head injury in World War II that left a metal plate in his head. Because of his diminished mental capacity, he acts in a childlike manner and believes that he is the Angel Gabriel, waiting for St. Peter to open the gates of Heaven for all of the saved. Troy used Gabe's disability check from the army to buy the house in which the play takes place. At the time of the play, Gabe has moved into his own apartment, a fact that weighs on Troy.

Jim Bono

Bono is Troy's best friend and drinking buddy. Several scenes of the play revolve around Troy and Bono's conversations in Troy's backyard while drinking on Friday nights. Troy met Bono while in prison. Bono both remembers Troy's past and serves as a moral compass for Troy in his relationship with his wife, Rose.

Lyons Maxson

Lyons is Troy's eldest son, fathered with his first wife. Lyons works as a jazz musician in Pittsburgh but often has a hard time making ends meet. Lyons often appears on Fridays, Troy's payday, to ask for money. Troy's complicated relationship with Lyons encompasses his admiration for his son's attempt to do something he loves with his life, but contempt for his refusal to be a breadwinner and responsible head of household.

Cory Maxson

Cory is the son of Troy and Rose. Cory has a relationship of conflict and violence with Troy. He believes that Troy is trying to hold him back in life by refusing to sign papers that would allow him to go to college on a football scholarship. Troy insists that Cory get a real job and be responsible. In the play's final scenes, Cory is kicked out of Troy's house after a violent struggle, only reluctantly returning eight years later for Troy's funeral.

Raynell Maxson

Raynell is Troy's daughter, fathered out of wedlock with Alberta, Troy's mistress. Alberta dies in childbirth and leaves Troy to raise Raynell. Rose agrees to raise his husband's daughter for her sake, not for his. The audience only sees Raynell as an infant and then as a small girl just before Troy's funeral.

Major Themes

The Creation of Order

The overarching theme of the play, alluded to in the title, is the idea of the creation of order - a fence is not a barrier in this reading, but a way to compartmentalize the world into understandable, manageable chunks. Troy Maxson is chiefly responsible for this desire for order, though for a different reason his wife Rose also craves it. Troy is caught in a world in which he feels he does not belong. He carries with him the scars, oppression, and disorder of his Southern childhood, the abuse of his father, and an unwelcome Pittsburgh. On the other hand, he is also a part of the growing African American middle class. He is promoted for a job he feels he does not deserve and he is unable to accept the idea that his children might have the freedom to create their own lives. For Troy, a fence is a way to section off part of the world as his own - his desire for a fence is a desire to find his place in the time and culture of twentieth century America.

The American Dream

Troy Maxson is the embodiment of an African-American generation, growing up in the post-World War II era, that finds itself finally able to realize the American ideal of life, liberty, and the pursuit of happiness. Troy has become more successful than his father, who remained a poor sharecropper and never owned his own land or property but, instead, paid all his wages and his life to an unjust land owner. Troy has bought his own house (though he feels guilty about the methods of payment). And in his sexual relationships he has embodied the freedom of a man to follow his own desires in a pursuit of happiness. Troy Maxson embraces his desire to be an individual.

This pursuit of the American Dream, however, is not without conflict. Troy cannot envision a generation doing more than his own accomplished. He cannot imagine his son achieving an even greater dream, and he cannot imagine a life unburdened by responsibility to family. In this way, Troy remains chained to his expectations of what a man can accomplish in the world.

African American Difference

In *Fences*, as well in his other plays, August Wilson seeks to point out the idea of difference between races and culture more than the monocultural ideal of sameness. The Civil Rights era of the 1960's and '70's can be broadly construed as African American's struggle for the same rights as whites. By the 1980's, Wilson saw this struggle for equality morphing into a culture that was attempting to erase the differences between races and peoples. African Americans, according to Wilson, were different than whites or any other races. They have their own distinct culture, history, and society. No people should have to become part of the majority culture just to enjoy the majority's rights and privileges.

Maintaining this difference is painful, and often destructive, as *Fences* shows. In his son Corey, Troy sees a generation that not only aspires for their own success in the world but also seeks to fold themselves into the white culture of the day. Sports is a metaphor for this; while Troy is bitter at losing his chance to play in an integrated Major Leagues, he still idealizes the Negro Leagues as symbol of African American pride. When Corey seeks a college scholarship to play football, Troy fears that his son will lose the difference of his race in his drive for success. This conflict of difference ultimately, and perhaps necessarily, destroys their relationship.

The Ideal of Responsibility

Troy Maxson is a man who takes seriously his responsibility for his family. His seriousness also becomes his greatest liability. Troy is a man caught between his own desire for freedom, embodied in his affair with Alberta and his fathering of an illegitimate child, and his fierce sense of loyalty to his wife, children, and brother.

Troy's sense of responsibility comes from his own father's bitter care for him and his siblings. His father's loyalty to his family can be seen as poisonous; his father's betrayal poisons his own relationship with Corey. Ultimately, Troy becomes his father. He abandons Rose for another woman and stubbornly refuses to repent for his sins. He also abandons his own brother and son, severing his relationships in his own quest for freedom. Troy demonstrates the idea that responsibility becomes as much a liability as a virtue.

Personal Apocalypse

Troy's brother Gabriel is a symbol of the personal apocalypse of Troy Maxson. Apocalypse, in its original meaning, connotes a revelation, or an understanding of the world that brings about some kind of ending. In *Fences*, Troy's struggles with his family and with his sense of purpose reveal to him the nature of death and the impermanence of his own life. Gabriel, thinking that he is the literal angel Gabriel, foretells this revelation in Troy's life. He insists that Troy's life is written in St. Peter's book, though his mortality is not a concept of which Troy can conceive. The tragedies of Troy's life serve as a series of death events; the abandonment by his father, his own abandonment of his son, the death of his lover, and ultimately the end of his own life all remind Troy that he is not in control of his own life, even as he attempts to control everyone around him.

Changing African American Culture

August Wilson's "Pittsburgh Cycle" portrays African American life in Pittsburgh during each decade of the twentieth century. *Fences* resonated with audiences partly because it so accurately captured the unique situation of African Americans during the 1950's and '60's. This was a time of great change for African American culture. The Civil Rights movement was in its nascent stages. African Americans were slowly moving into a respectable middle class and out of the destitute poverty of the late nineteenth and early twentieth centuries. The post-World War II generation was first embracing the ideal of personal freedom.

There are several instances of this changing culture in *Fences*. One is Troy's own advancement in his job. Troy is a trash collector, a seemingly undesirable job, yet his promotion to truck driver bestows on him a level of authority and purpose that he feels he has otherwise not achieved in his life. His discomfort with his own advancement is seen in his desire to retire shortly after getting his raise. This changing culture also creates bitterness in Troy. This is seen in his love/hate relationship with the game of baseball. On the one hand, Troy loves the game for the identity that it once gave him; on the other hand, he despises the game for its segregation and for robbing him of his chance at greatness. Troy is caught in the changing culture and represents a generation lost in their understanding of the world around them.

Freedom vs. Protection

The fence in August Wilson's play serves as a symbol of conflicting desires. In one sense, Troy and Rose seek to build a fence to keep the world out of their lives. Rose's desire for a fence symbolizes the way in which she seeks to protect her family. She knows that Troy's checkered past is always there and that he is, perhaps, only moments away from making decisions that forever affect her and her child. Rose's fence seeks to keep the family in and the dangerous world out. It is a symbol of protection.

Though Troy seeks to protect his family and his way of life, the fence also becomes a symbol of discontent in his own life. In his confrontation with Rose, Troy exclaims that he has spent his whole life providing for the family. He has been the protector and defender of a quiet, normal life. The fence, therefore, does not protect Troy but instead keeps him from achieving his ultimate desire for individuality and self actualization.

Glossary of Terms

A&P

The A&P, the Great Atlantic and Pacific Tea Company, is a grocery store chain on the Eastern seaboard of the United States.

Angel Gabriel

In the Bible, the archangel Gabriel is God's messenger to earth.

atavistic

Atavism is the tendency to return to an ancestral type.

Aunt Jemimah

Aunt Jemimah is a logo character used for a brand of pancakes and syrups. She is a stereotypical depiction of an Old South mammy.

blues

Blues music is a form of music and a genre of music developed in African American communities in the late nineteenth and early twentieth centuries. Blues combines spirituals, gospel, and field songs into rhymed narrative ballads.

Hellhounds

In religious folklore, hellhounds guard the gates of hell and are responsible for dragging souls into it.

Jackie Robinson

Jackie Robinson was the first African American player to play in baseball's white Major Leagues in 1947.

Negro Leagues

The Negro Leagues were professional leagues of baseball for African American players before Major League baseball's integration.

numbers

The numbers is a kind of lottery game of chance.

Pearly Gates

The gates of heaven.

Penitentiary

A penitentiary is a prison.

Pigfeet

Pigfeet is a dish associated with Southern Style cooking and the African American soul food tradition.

Pirates

The Pittsburgh Pirates are the Major League baseball team for the city of Pittsburgh, Pennsylvania.

recruitment

Recruiting is the process of giving college scholarships to high school students to play a specific sport for that college.

Satchel Paige

Satchel Paige was a pitcher in baseball's Negro Leagues. He is widely believed to be one of the best all time pitchers in baseball, though he was only able to pitch in the Major Leagues as an older player.

soft wood

Soft wood is a type of wood, such as pine wood, used for construction.

spikes

Spikes are a type of special shoe worn by athletes in order to improve foot hold on the playing field.

St. Peter

In religious folklore, St. Peter guards the gates of heaven and keeps a book with the names of all those that are to be allowed in.

stroking

A crude reference to sexual intercourse.

the World Series

The World Series is a series of championship games in Major League baseball.

Short Summary

The play begins in 1957. Troy Maxson and his friend Jim Bono share stories and a bottle of whiskey on a Friday night. Troy's wife, Rose, tells Troy that their son Cory is being recruited to play college football. Troy is disgusted with the idea. Troy had once been a star in the Negro Leagues, but he was heartbroken by his barrier from the majors. He sees no better future in sports for his son. His older son Lyons stops by to ask his father for money; Troy is not pleased that Lyons is a struggling musician, but he accepts that Lyons is his own man and is making his own way in life.

The next day Troy and Rose get into an argument over his son's apparent laziness. Rose tells him that he has gone to football practice. Gabriel Maxson enters. He is Troy's brother. Gabe suffered a head injury in World War II and now believes he is the angel Gabriel. He carries a trumpet around his neck to blow and open the gates of heaven. Gabe has recently moved out of Troy's house and into his own apartment, something he is very proud of. It is soon learned that Troy used Gabe's disability wages from the Army to buy his house.

A few hours later, Cory returns from football practice. Rose tells him that Troy is furious that he did not help him build the fence in the yard. Their conversation turns contentious after Troy asks Cory about his football scholarship and his job at the A&P. Troy demands that he quit the team and get back his job at the grocery store. After Cory leaves, Troy tells Rose that he doesn't want his son to be like him in any way. She tells Troy that Cory just wants to hear that he has done a good job, but Troy says he can give no more than he already does to his family.

Two weeks later, Troy and Bono come home from work and report how Troy confronted his boss and received a promotion to be the driver of the garbage truck. Troy tells the story of his own father, and how his father beat him and kicked him out of the house at fourteen years old. Troy hates his father but respects his sense of responsibility to his family. After coming to Pittsburgh as a young man, Troy killed a man while trying to rob him and went to prison for fifteen years. This is when Lyons was born. Cory returns from his football practice and is upset because his coach told him he couldn't play. Cory knows that Troy went to the coach to have him kicked off the team. He and his father argue, and Troy tells him that he shouldn't strike out with him.

The next morning, Cory stands by the tree in the yard and practices his baseball swing, but he is more awkward than his father. Troy returns from the police station after having been called to bail out Gabe for disorderly conduct. Bono and Troy begin to build the fence and Bono chides Troy for his scandalous relationship with a woman named Alberta. Bono implores Troy to hang onto Rose. When Bono leaves, Troy admits to Rose that he is having an affair and that he is fathering an illegitimate child. Rose tries to explain how she worked to be a good wife and mother to him and his child. Troy insists that he has done nothing wrong except follow his own desire. She tells Troy that he takes a lot from her and this makes him angry. He goes towards Rose and Cory steps in and shoves Troy. Troy almost retaliates violently before Rose stops him and Troy tells Cory not to strike out.

Six months pass by. Troy is going to see his newborn child when the hospital calls - Alberta has died in childbirth. Troy is enraged and begins engaging a personified Death in conversation. He assures death that he will closely guard everything that belongs to him. A few days later, Troy comes home with his baby in his arms. He pleads with Rose to care for the child even while he remains unapologetic for his infidelity. Rose accepts the child but rejects Troy.

Two more months pass by. Cory has graduated and is now looking for a job. Troy initiates a confrontation with him. Cory tells Troy that he doesn't count in the house anymore. They have a physical fight and Troy wrestles the baseball bat away from Cory. Instead of hitting him, Troy kicks him out of the house. As Cory leaves, Troy again taunts death.

Eight years pass. It is 1965 and Rose, Lyons, and Bono gather in the Maxson home for Troy's funeral. Rose has been raising Raynell, Troy's daughter. Cory comes into the yard dressed in a Marine's uniform. It is the first time he has been home in eight years. He and Raynell sit on the front porch and sing Troy's old blues song about his dog, Blue. Cory tells Rose that he is not going to Troy's funeral but Rose tells him he must make peace with his father now.

Gabe enters the yard. It had been uncertain as to whether the mental institution where he lives would let him come, but he arrives with his trumpet, ready to blow Troy into heaven. He tries to blow the trumpet but no sound comes out. Undeterred, Gabe starts to dance, pushing Lyons away from him. As he dances, the gates of heaven open for Troy and Gabe tells them all, "That's the way that go!"

Quotes and Analysis

"You and me is two different people, Pop."

Fences, 18

This line is spoken by Troy's oldest son, Lyons. Troy chides Lyons for being lazy and poor and for not wanting to get a real job in the sanitation department or with some other company. Lyons spends his nights in the jazz clubs as a musician. Troy, however, has only a limited say in how Lyons lives his life because Lyons was raised by his mother while Troy was in jail. Though Troy teases his oldest son, the audience sees that Troy begrudgingly respects his son for being his own man and for doing what he loves even at the expense of stability. It is a choice that Troy feels he was never able to make.

"You go on and get your book-learning so you can work yourself up in that A&P or learn how to fix cars or build houses or something, get you a trade. That way you have something can't nobody take away from you.

Fences, 35

Troy speaks this line to his youngest son, Cory, as they work together to build the fence that Rose has been asking for around their yard. Troy is troubled by Cory's interest in sports and the opportunity that he is being given to play football on scholarship at a college. Troy feels that his own years playing professional baseball in the Negro Leagues was time wasted; that the white powers of control conspired against him and prevented him from being recognized as the great player that he was. In response to this disappointment, Troy demands that his son give up a dream that he believes will only break his heart.

"Cory: How come you ain't never liked me?

Troy: Liked you? Who the hell say I got to like you?"

Fences, 37

In this conversation between father and son, Cory unearths Troy's deep seeded emotions towards his family. Though he does love his family, and his tenderness and concern are on display in other scenes, Troy has come to a point in his life where he finally becomes broken by the responsibility of caring for them. Responsibility, in Troy's world, is the most noble calling of a man. This responsibility, however, has caused Troy to become a bitter man. He cannot "like" his son because of his own desire that Cory not become like him.

"(He sings.) Hear it ring! Hear it ring! I had a dog his name was Blue...You know Blue was mighty true."

Fences, 44

This is a line from a song that Troy created about his childhood dog, Blue. Troy feels a special kindred to this old dog because it licked and cared for him after his father beat him and kicked him out of the house as a child. Troy took his dog north with him and, in a sense, Troy loved Old Blue more than anyone because the dog exemplified traits of loyalty and dedication to which Troy aspired. Old Blue becomes a metaphor for Troy's own failings as a husband and father. In the play's final scene, Cory and Raynell eulogize their dead father by singing of Blue's redemption in heaven.

Some people build fences to keep people out...and other people build fences to keep people in.

Fences, 61

This line occurs during a conversation between Troy and his friend Bono. Here, Bono succinctly sums up the overarching metaphor of the play. Though Troy initially asks why Rose would want to build a physical fence, Bono understands the symbolic importance. Rose builds her symbolic fence to keep her husband and her son together. She attempts to keep her family inside the home. Troy, on the other hand, builds symbolic fences of dedication and responsibility, aspirations so high that neither he nor his sons can live up to them. These fences push people away and, in the end, Troy loses his wife and son because of the lofty standards he cannot reach.

"Got me two rooms. In the basement. Got my own door too. Wanna see my key? ...That's my own key! Ain't nobody else got a key like that."

Fences, 25

This line is spoken by Troy's brother, Gabriel Maxson, during the play's first act. Gabriel represents Troy's conflict over protecting the ones he loves and giving them their freedom. Gabriel, like Troy, is concerned with being his own man and controlling his own destiny, which is why he moved out of Troy's house. However, Gabriel was wounded in World War II and is disabled to the point where he is unable to care for himself. Troy and Gabe's relationship becomes tragic as Troy sells out Gabriel, sending him to a mental hospital and taking his monthly disability checks from the government to support his own family.

"Alright...Mr. Death. See now...I'm gonna tell you what I'm gonna do. I'm gonna take and build me a fence around this yard. See? I'm gonna build me a fence around what belongs to me. And then I want you to stay on the other side. See? You stay over there until you're ready for me. Then you come on. Bring your army. Bring your sickle."

Fences, 77

This quote, spoken by Troy after he hears the news that his mistress has died giving birth to his daughter, is a reminder to the audience that Troy's struggle is not just with his son or his wife but also with forces beyond his own earthly power. Wilson uses archetypal themes from classical Greek theater to depict the struggles of Troy Maxson. In this case, it is the struggle between heaven and hell over the soul of one man. Troy is in a constant battle with death throughout his entire life. It is a battle for his own destiny and the right to control his own fate.

"Your daddy wanted you to be everything he wasn't...and at the same time he tried to make you into everything he was. I don't know if he was right or wrong...but I do know he meant to do more good than he meant to do harm."

Fences, 97

Rose Maxson speaks these lines to her son Cory after Troy's death. Cory struggles with being released from his father's hold. Cory finds that his father's control extends beyond the grave. In this scene, Rose attempts to offer some measure of redemption for her husband. Here, she sums up Troy's conflicting relationship with his sons. He strongly desired that his sons not be forced to endure the disappointment that he himself faced during his life, yet he also could not stand for Cory, the boy he raised, to overtake him as patriarch.

"I wanted a house that I could sing in. And that's what your daddy gave me. I didn't know to keep up his strength I had to give up little pieces of mine...It was my choice. It was my life and I didn't have to live it like that. But that's what life offered me in the way of being a woman and I took it."

Fences, 98

Rose Maxson, who speaks these lines in the play's final scene, is contradictorily a figure of repressed femininity and also a figure of great feminine strength. She admits in this scene that her life as a housewife and mother was forced upon her by Troy, yet she insists that at no point did she ever lose her ability to choose. The domestic life was what she chose and in this scene she owns that choice for herself. Some of the play's critics have noted that Rose is the least dimensional of Wilson's characters, but this scene shows that glimpses of Rose's complexity are able to come through.

"That's the way that go!"

Fences, 101

Gabriel Maxson speaks the play's final line. After Troy dies, Gabriel shows up at the house with his trumpet, ready to "tell St. Peter to open the gates." As he tries to blow his trumpet, no sound comes out and Gabriel begins a strange dance. It is a dance of grief and trauma but also a foolish dance. Wilson turns the traditional ending of the play on its head; the protagonist, Troy, does not have the play's final word. Instead, it is the "fool," Gabriel, who ends the play with a simple declaration that fate has finally taken its man. Gabriel does not let anything keep him from redeeming his brother and sending him into heaven.

Summary and Analysis of Act I, scene 1

Summary

Troy Maxson and Jim Bono are talking and drinking in the yard on a Friday night. Troy is concerned about his job at the sanitation department because he asked the bosses why the colored men have to lift the rubbish cans while the white men drive the truck. Bono asks about a girl, Alberta, with whom Troy has been flirting, and reprimands him for not being completely faithful to his wife, Rose. Troy replies, "I eye all the women…Don't never let nobody tell you Troy Maxson don't eye the women." Troy describes Alberta as "one of them Florida gals. They got some healthy women down there…Got a little bit of Indian in her."

Rose Maxson enters and she and Troy reminisce about how she won him for a husband though he hadn't been a marrying type. They argue about shopping at the A&P, which is cheaper, or at the local shop Bella's, which is a part of the community. Rose reports that a college football team is recruiting their son Cory. Troy wants Cory to give up on football because the white man will never let him get anywhere with it. He believes that Cory should keep the job he has at the A&P and "get recruited in how to fix cars or something where he can make a living."

Troy played baseball in his youth, but it was before the days of Jackie Robinson and baseball's integration. Troy couldn't advance to the big leagues because of his race. Baseball, Troy says, never got him anywhere. "Ain't got a pot to piss in or a window to throw it out of" because of the sport. Bono replies that the sports have changed and that many African-Americans are playing in the major leagues now, but Troy answers that minorities will never receive the same deference given to white players.

Rose reprimands Troy for drinking so much, and Troy chides her. He tells them both that they cannot teach him anything about death. "Death ain't nothing but a fastball on the outside corner…That's all death is to me." He relates a story of how he caught pneumonia in July of 1941 and was sent to the hospital. He says that he struggled with death for three days and eventually won the wrestling contest. Troy refuses to go easy; Death will have to fight to get him in the end.

Lyons, Troy's son, comes by to ask Troy for money. Lyons is a struggling jazz musician, "more caught up in the rituals and 'idea' of being a musician than in the actual practice of the music." Troy knows that Lyons is coming to ask him for money and teases him in a mean-spirited way. Lyons asks for ten dollars and Troy refuses to directly give it to him, making him take the money from Rose instead. Lyons insists that his girlfriend, Bonnie, is working at one of the hospitals and that he will have the money to pay Troy back.

Troy tells of buying his furniture on credit from a mysterious white man who may or may not have been the devil. He tells him that he pays ten dollars to the devil each month for the furniture and that he has been paying that sum for the last fifteen years. Rose shakes her head and calls it a tall tale. Troy insists that his son get a job and offers to get him in with the sanitation department. Lyons says the work wouldn't agree with him and that he is going to keep making music because it gives his life meaning. He tells Troy, "You and me is two different people, Pop." Troy tells them he doesn't have extra money since his brother, Gabe, moved out of the house.

Lyons leaves and Bono tells Troy that Lyons will "be alright...The boy is still young." Troy tells Bono, "The *boy* is thirty-four years old." Troy goes to Rose and tells Bono he loves her so much that it hurts him. He says he's run out of ways to love her and that Bono shouldn't come by his house on "Monday morning talking about time to go to work...'cause I'm still gonna be stroking!"

Analysis

The play's title is a manifestation of its primary theme: the ways that people protect themselves from forces bigger and more powerful than themselves, yet also trap those they love into relationships of conflict. Each character in the play attempts to create their own emotional fence to control others and protect themselves from those they love most. Though the play is meant to give a realistic picture of life in the industrial north of the 1950's, the themes of *Fences* are also meant to be universal for all audiences.

Wilson spends much of the first scene establishing the characters, their relationships, and the world of black working-class Pittsburgh. This scene introduces the play's protagonist, Troy Maxson. Troy is a man of many layers. He is a devoted husband and father, though as we learn he is also controlling and unfaithful. He is forward thinking – he fights for equality and his job and he pursues the American Dream – yet he also feels helpless in a world that seems to be passing him by. Most importantly, perhaps, he is a man that wants his children to have everything he did not, yet cannot seem to stand the idea that they would bypass the hardships that he had to go through.

Jim Bono is Troy's closest friend and confidant. It is noteworthy that Troy says the words "I love you" to Bono, but not to his sons. Bono is Wilson's representation of African American brotherhood and their close relationship explores how masculine bonding creates an intimacy not shared with family. Rose Maxson, Troy's wife, is the epitome of this intimate divide. Rose represents the choices (and lack thereof) for African American women in 1957. She has the inner strength to love Troy and to care for his children even in the face of Troy's unfaithfulness, but she can never define herself outside the boundaries of family.

Troy's sons act as a mirror of his best and worst qualities. Lyons Maxson, Troy's oldest, is a jazz musician. He is laid back and unconcerned with daily problems. His is a much different life than Troy's, but Troy begrudgingly respects Lyons for rejecting the proscriptions of society. Cory, introduced in the second scene, is the truest representation of the conflict between father and son, a dominant theme throughout the play.

Troy's relationship with Rose and Bono and his relationship with his sons is a study in contrast. In this early scene, Troy enters the play as a clown. He makes crude and funny sexual advances towards his wife and he jovially drinks and gossips with his friend Bono. When Lyons appears, however, the conflict between father and son becomes apparent. Troy might somehow admire Lyons' choices in life, but it is only because he has no control over his son. The audience later finds out that Troy spent most of Lyons' childhood in prison. Now, he can only be a spectator as Lyons lives his life. Though Troy does not approve of his son's lifestyle, he understands that Lyons can only do what he wants to do. Troy's issue with loaning Lyons money symbolizes this. Troy knows that his ten dollars will only go to support his son's jazz career and so he gives him a hard time about it. In the end, Lyons gets the money circuitously through Rose because Troy cannot help but support his son. Lyons' declaration that jazz music gives his life meaning is powerful for Troy since he feels that his life has had no other meaning beyond responsibility for others.

This scene first introduces the play's motif of death. Here, death appears in Troy's story of owing money to a furniture company. Death is a devil who appears as a white man selling furniture. This story is Troy's way of symbolizing his own concept of racism during his life. Though he does not actually owe any money to a white man (as his father had as a sharecropper), Troy still feels that his life is somehow indebted to forces that he cannot understand or clearly perceive. In this way, he will always be in debt and will continually struggle with death.

Summary and Analysis of Act I, scene 2

Summary

It is Saturday morning. The scene begins with Rose singing softly, "Jesus, be a fence all around me every day / Jesus, I want you to protect me as a I travel / on my way." Troy is grumbling about people who play the lottery and people who squander their winnings. He is especially disdainful of a black man named Pope who won a large sum in the lottery and used it to finance a restaurant. Troy feels as though Pope has sold out the black community by giving poor service to his black clientele while catering to white people. The numbers, Troy says, "Ain't done nothing but make a worser fool out of him than he was before."

He grumbles about Cory being lazy. Rose tells him that Cory went to football practice, but Troy swears he only wanted to avoid working on building the fence in their yard. Troy insists that Cory "ain't done a lick of work in his life." Rose tells Troy to go back into the house and get a new cup of coffee to correct his mood. Troy grumbles that he is the one to always take the blame for other people's shortcomings.

Gabriel enters, singing. Gabe is Troy's brother. He is mentally disabled because of an injury suffered as a soldier in World War II. He now has a metal plate in his head. Gabe believes that he is the archangel Gabriel. He carries a trumpet on a string around his neck. He says that St. Peter has Troy's name in his book in heaven and Gabe is prepared to blow the trumpet to announce the coming of heaven to earth.

Gabe sells fruit out of a basket for extra money and is always proud of the few quarters he is able to collect from those that feel sorry for him. Gabe feels that Troy is always mad at him for some reason, though Troy denies this. Gabe asks Troy if he is mad at him for moving to Miss Pearl's house. He tells Troy, "I just moved over to Miss Pearl's to keep out from in your way. I ain't mean no by it." Gabe, however, is proud of his room and his independence.

Rose offers Gabe breakfast, but he says that "Aunt Jemimah" came by and cooked him "a whole mess of flapjacks." He shows Troy his quarters and tells him that he is going to buy a new horn to announce the opening of heaven's gates. He tells Troy that he hears the "hellhounds" and that he has to chase them away. Gabe runs off to chase the noise that he believes he hears.

Rose is concerned that Gabe isn't eating right in his new lodgings. Troy says he has done all he could for Gabe and that he does not deserve to be in some state hospital. Troy is concerned for Gabe's freedom, wishing him to live a peaceful life after what happened to him in the war. "Man go over there and fight the war...messin' around with them Japs, get half his head blown off...and they give him a lousy three thousand dollars. And I had to swoop down on that."

Rose doesn't want Troy to go into the controversy over the money, but Troy reminds her that it is only because of Gabe's three thousand dollars that he was able to buy the house they now live in. It is apparent that Troy feels a measure of guilt over using the money for the house, though his intentions were clearly noble; he wanted to take care of his brother and provide a place for him to live. That Gabe has now moved out of the house for which he paid is another source of Troy's guilt. He tells Rose that if it weren't for Gabe's monthly disability checks, "I wouldn't have a pot to piss in or a window to throw it out of. And I'm fifty-three years old. Now see if you can understand that!" Troy leaves the yard to go to the Taylors' house and listen to the ball game.

Analysis

This scene begins with Rose singing an African American spiritual representing the metaphor of the play. Rose sings, "Jesus, be a fence all around me every day / Jesus, I want you to protect me as I travel…." This song combines the uniqueness of the African American religious experience with Rose's domestic desire to establish a safe and happy home with her husband and son. There is an historic tradition in African American religion of travel and movement. Eighteenth and nineteenth century Southern black slaves often identified with the exodus of the Hebrew Bible. *Fences*, however, is a play about the tension between this historic value of exodus and the mid-twentieth century American ideal of settling into a home with a family. In this opening scene, Rose's song is an outer expression of an inner conflict.

The dialogue between Rose and Troy regarding gambling and Cory's work ethic is an example of the value that Troy puts on self-reliance and responsibility. Troy is openly disdainful of another man in the neighborhood who benefited from playing the lottery. He is unable to appreciate the fact that the man is attempting to better his life through his luck, even though both he and Rose know he is technically correct in his diagnosis of the social ill of "the numbers." There is an association for Troy in gambling and in Cory's scholarship to play football. Troy sees both games as a person's loss of control over his own destiny. It is a mistake that Troy decides never to make again and one he does not want for his son.

This scene introduces Gabriel, Troy's brother who is disabled after losing part of his head in battle during World War II. Gabriel is a "spectacle character." His belief that he is the angel Gabriel is meant to be humorous for the audience, even as he gains sympathy for how his life and right mind were taken from him. Gabriel, however, does not just serve comic purposes; instead, he is a part of the story and provides an intriguing sub-plot. Like Troy, Gabriel is concerned with his freedom and independence. He has moved out of Troy's house and is trying to make it on his own, even though he can only peddle fruit on the street.

Gabriel, besides playing the role of clown to provide some measure of comic relief, also functions as a kind of Greek chorus. In ancient Greek literature, a chorus was a group of characters that provided background and summary information to the audience in order to show them how they should react to a particular moment of the play. In some classical plays, the chorus was directly involved with the characters in the play, providing them crucial pieces of the story not evident from their point of view. Gabriel functions in a similar way in Wilson's play. He brings a back story (as a soldier) of contributing the ultimate act of responsibility and sacrifice -- giving his life to his country. His presence is also a constant reminder to Troy that larger forces are at work in his life and that he is not always in control.

Troy loves and respects his brother, yet the audience learns that the relationship is more complicated. Troy took Gabe's initial disability payout from the government and built a house with the intention of he, his wife, and Gabe living there. He also continues to take Gabe' s monthly government check for expenses. Now that Gabe has moved out, Troy faces the reality that once again he is unable to provide fully for his family without the help of his disabled brother. Because of Gabe's presence, the audience slowly learns that Troy is not the all-powerful patriarch that he claims to be.

Summary and Analysis of Act I, scene 3

Summary

Scene three opens four hours later. Rose is hanging laundry on the line and Cory comes in from his football practice. Rose warns him that Troy "like to had a fit with you running out of here this morning without doing your chores." Cory asks if Rose told Troy about the recruiter and Rose says that she did but that Troy "ain't said nothing too much." Rose insists that he go and start his chores and make some lunch.

Troy enters the yard and sneaks up on Rose, scaring her. He is very affectionate with Rose and makes some comical sexual advances, but Rose tells him, "Go on…I ain't studying you." Troy calls for Cory and then picks up a board, starting to saw and build the fence. When Cory comes out, Troy demands to know why he had not finished his chores before leaving the house that morning. Cory doesn't answer but only picks up a board and begins to saw.

Cory asks his father why he doesn't own a TV. Troy is incredulous over this question but Cory insists, "Everybody got one…They got lots of things on TV. Baseball games and everything. We could watch the World Series." Troy wants to know how much a TV costs and Cory replies they are two hundred dollars and "That ain't much, Pop." Sarcastically, Troy tells him, "Naw, it's just two hundred dollars." He points to the roof of the house and explains how it has been ten years since the roof was tarred. When the snow comes, it will seep inside. The moisture will rot the wood and soon it will be leaking all over them. He asks Cory how much he thinks a roof costs, but Cory doesn't know. Troy tells him, "Two hundred and sixty-four dollars…cash money. While you thinking about a TV, I got to be thinking about the roof...."

Cory insists that Troy isn't as poor as he makes out to be, but Troy tells Cory that all he has to his name is seventy-three dollars and twenty-two cents in the bank. Cory tells him he could put the TV on credit, but Troy says, "I ain't gonna owe nobody nothing if I can help it. Miss a payment and they come and snatch it right out your house." He cuts Cory a deal; if he can get a hundred dollars he will put the other hundred down on a TV. Cory insists he will show his father that he can get the money.

Cory changes the subject to talking about the Pirates, Pittsburgh's baseball team. Troy says that he doesn't think about the Pirates because they have an all white team except for "that Puerto Rican boy…Clemente." Cory tries to convince Troy that black players such as Hank Aaron and Wes Covington are playing more in the big leagues, but Troy dismisses this idea. He tells Cory that he could hit forty-three home runs just like Hank Aaron right now. Cory insists he couldn't and Troy says, "We had better pitching in the Negro leagues. I hit seven home runs off of Satchel Paige. You can't get no better than that." He tells Cory that he is done talking about the subject.

Troy changes the subject to Cory and asks him if he is being recruited by a school to play football and Cory tells him he is. Troy will have to sign the permission papers in order for him to be recruited. Troy wonders why Cory isn't working at his job at the A&P instead, and Cory tells him, "Mr. Stawicki say he gonna hold my job for me until after the football season" and that he is going to work weekends instead. Troy tells him, "ain't no need for nobody coming around here to talk to me about signing nothing...The white man ain't gonna let you get nowhere with that football noway. You go on and get your book-learnings so you can work yourself up in that A&P or learn how to fix cars or build houses or something, get you a trade. That way you have something can't nobody take away from you."

Distraught, Cory tells Troy that someone else has already gotten his old job at the A&P. Troy tells Cory that he is a "fool...to let somebody take away your job so you can play some football." The two have a contentious back-and-forth over Cory not calling Troy "sir," and Troy asserts his authority over the boy: "Nigger, as long as you in my house, you put that sir on the end of it when you talk to me!" Troy reminds him that he takes his responsibility to his family seriously, that he works hard and puts "up with them crackers every day" in order to do so. He orders Cory to go back down to the A&P and get his job back.

Cory leaves and Rose returns after overhearing the conversation. Troy tells her, "I don't want him to be like me! I want him to move as far away from my life as he can get." This means moving away from sports, but Rose implores him to admit that the reason he was excluded from playing in the major leagues after integration was because he was too old. Rose tells Troy, "Everything that boy do...he do for you. He wants you to way 'Good job, son.' That's all." Rose tells him that times have moved on and that the world has changed, but Troy insists that he's only doing the best he can by giving all his sweat and blood to support the family. "That's all I got, Rose. That's all I got to give," he tells her.

Analysis

Troy and Cory's conversation about the television set is both an example of father-son bonding and a sign of just how much the world is moving on without Troy. The television set is a symbol of the success of modernity and the ability of African Americans during this time to advance (however limited those advancements might be) in social and economic ways.

The television, as Cory describes it, is fundamentally changing how people interact with the world. His argument that "they got lots of things on TV" is his way of telling Troy that the world outside of Pittsburgh is much bigger than Troy remembers it. It is recognition that the world has changed and continues to be changed. Cory understands his own future is dependent on Troy's understanding of this change and being able to convince him of this is paramount if Cory is to ever play football in college.

Troy, however, is resistant to the idea of the television. It is not just that he fears the world's advancement, but it is also that he does not quite understand it and refuses to deal with it. Troy prefers to keep his thoughts on the domestic scene. He reminds Cory that the price of the TV is almost what it would take to re-tar the roof. Troy uses the example of the TV to shame Cory for not taking his own domestic responsibility seriously. A conversation that begins as a simple father-son lesson in economics turns into an argument in which Troy fights to strip his son of his future manhood and Cory further develops his deep hatred of his father.

The argument between Cory and Troy in this scene also reveals Troy's deep disappointment with his own sports career. The audience begins to see that this, in part, is one reason Troy is so obstinate about signing a paper for Cory's scholarship recruitment. Troy played in the Negro Leagues, the segregated baseball league, and he boasts to his son that he and his teammates back then were better than almost all of the white or black major leaguers of the present. Troy feels as though he never really got his chance to show his true talents to the world. He can find no specific cause and so develops his own deep mistrust of the power held over African Americans by white America.

This distrust is what fuels the passion in one of the key scenes of the play. After arguing that Cory should get his "book-learning" so that he "can work…up in that A&P or learn how to fix cars or build houses" instead of playing football (which Troy obviously sees his son is passionate about), Cory asks his father why he never liked him. Troy is surprised by the question and, instead of answering in a loving way, becomes cruel and militaristic with his son. He demands to know what law says he has to like him. Troy's life lesson to his son is valid -- a person must accept the responsibilities given to them -- but his delivery of this advice is hurtful to both Cory and Rose and further alienates them from him.

Summary and Analysis of Act I, scene 4

Summary

It is two weeks later. The phone rings and Cory picks it up and has a conversation about his football spikes with a friend on the other end of the line. Cory is in a rush to get to the football game, and Rose implores him to clean his room so that his father won't know he is out watching football. Cory leaves.

Troy and Bono enter talking about Troy's confrontation with Mr. Rand, his boss at the sanitation department. Troy had gone to the union with his complaint over not being allowed to drive the garbage truck. Bono was sure that Troy would get fired over the incident, but instead Mr. Rand had been forced to let Troy drive the truck. Troy calls Rose and teases her that, "You supposed to come when I call you, woman." Rose bristles at this and Troy tells her he once had an old dog named Blue that "used to get uppity like that." Rose reminisces that Troy used to sing about that old dog and that Cory used to sing with him. Troy recounts a verse of the song.

Lyons enters and Troy remarks that there was a story in the paper about how the police had raided Sefus', one of the clubs that Lyons plays music at. Lyons tells him that he has no part in the gambling going on there, and Troy only remarks, "They got some rogues…." Rose tells Lyons that his daddy got a promotion to drive the truck. Bono remarks that this would be a good thing "if the nigger knew how to *drive*…Been fighting with them people about driving and ain't even got a license." Troy is certain that he'll be able to work all that out.

Troy is sure that Lyons is about to ask for more money, but instead Lyons pulls out ten dollars and tries to pay Troy back. Troy tells Lyons that he should put the money in the bank and refuses to take it. Rose takes the money instead. Gabriel enters telling everyone they should get ready for the judgment day and gives Rose a rose. Lyons asks Gabe if he's been chasing hellhounds and fighting the devil and Gabe readily agrees that he has. Lyons tells them he has to get to his gig, and he asks if Troy would like to come down and hear him play. Troy tells him, "I don't like that Chinese music. All that noise."

Rose and Troy begin talking about Cory's recruitment and Lyons wants to know what school he is going to. Troy tells Bono that he went down to the A&P and talked to Cory's boss and that he knows Cory has been lying to him about getting his old job back. Lyons tells Troy that Cory is growing up and trying to fill his daddy's shoes. Bono tells the story of his own father, a drifter searching for the "New Land." He never stayed in one place long enough to actually be a father.

Troy reminisces about his own father. His father was a sharecropper raising eleven kids on his own. He was more worried about "getting them bales of cotton in to Mr. Lubin" than caring for his kids. Troy's mother left the children when Troy was young and never returned. His father didn't know how to do anything but farm, and though he was "good for nobody" he always felt a responsibility for his kids and made sure they had a roof over their heads and food in their mouths. Troy tells of how when he turned fourteen he started "sniffing around Joe Canewell's daughter." One afternoon, Troy left his plowing early and goes to the river and started "fooling around" with the girl by the river. His father found him and started beating him with leather straps, chasing him away. His father then tried to sleep with the girl himself. Troy saw this and started to fight his father. When his daddy faced him, he "could see why the devil had never come to get him…cause he was the devil himself." Troy's father beat him into unconsciousness and his old dog Blue woke him, licking his face. Troy left his house and "right there the world suddenly got big. And it was a long time before I could cut it down to where I could handle it." Troy says that he lost touch with all his family, except for Gabe, and that he hopes his father is dead.

Lyons tells his father that he didn't realize he had left home at fourteen years of age. Troy says that, at fourteen, he walked two hundred miles down to Mobile, where he caught a ride with a group of black men heading to Pittsburgh. They all thought they were heading towards freedom, but Troy found that conditions were even worse in Pittsburgh than they had been on the farm. Troy began to steal in order to survive and then was shot in the chest while trying to rob a man. Troy killed the man with a knife and was sent to prison for fifteen years. This is where he met Bono. Troy learned to play baseball in prison and he met Rose several years after that.

Lyons asks Troy to come down to the club and hear his music, but Troy refuses and finds several excuses not to go. After Lyons leaves, Troy puts his arm around Bono and tells him that he has known him longer than anyone else and that "a man can't ask for no more than that." Troy tells him that he loves him and Bono gives his love back, and departs.

Cory enters the yard, upset. He throws his football helmet on the ground and tells Rose that Troy went to his coach and told him Cory couldn't play football or get recruited. The coach wouldn't let Cory play. Cory is upset because "That was the one chance I had." Troy and Cory resume their argument over working at the A&P. Cory tells Troy that he is "scared I'm gonna be better than you...." Troy pulls Cory in close and tells him he has made a mistake; "you swung at the ball and didn't hit it. That's strike one…Don't you strike out!"

Analysis

This scene begins and ends with confrontation. The first confrontation is a fruitful one for Troy and his family while the final one further destroys the domestic threads holding the family together. Troy and Bono enter the yard recounting how Troy stood up to his boss, Mr. Rand, and has now become the first African American garbage truck driver in the Hill District of Pittsburgh. This is a good thing for the family since Troy will be able to work longer and bring in more pay. In a way, Troy can finally feel that his persistence in standing up to the unseen forces of the white world is now paying off for him like it never did during his baseball career.

Gabe, Lyons, and Rose join Troy in the yard and comprise his audience for the celebration. After speaking of his promotion, Troy moves on to a different story. He begins to recount the story of his father and how he became independent at the age of fourteen. He proudly tells the assembled group of his father's dedication to his family, even though he was a mean and bitter man. But his relationship with his father ended when his father had caught him having sex with a young girl and chased Troy away, only so that he could have her for himself. Troy fights his father, is beaten badly, and leaves home to begin his journey up north. Troy proudly feels as though he took what was best from his father – his sense of loyalty and dedication to his family. The irony is that Troy also has taken his father's bitterness and cruelty. It is not entirely clear if Troy realizes this.

Critics have argued that *Fences* is a story of manhood in modern America. Troy Maxson is meant to represent the African American experience of manhood, the contradictions and flaws inherent in this masculine process. There is first the question of the creation of the man; in Troy's experience, this is a fundamentally violent operation. It is meant to symbolize the birth of the self; Wilson portrays the African American creation of self as a process of violence no different in the 1950's than it had been for eighteenth and nineteenth century slaves.

The second stage of manhood is the continual way in which the African American man is measured against the ideal of the American Dream, an ideal that becomes increasingly materialistic during the middle decades of the twentieth century and increasingly illusory as well. This is another way to read Cory and Troy's conversation regarding the TV in the previous scene. Troy sees Cory accepting the idea that the accumulation of stuff creates desirable social status for the individual. Troy is deeply skeptical of this even though he implicitly understands it (he encourages Bono to buy his wife a refrigerator).

The solution to these problems of manhood, according to Troy, is to accept the world's inherent violence and to barricade oneself against any materialistic thing that might inculcate passivity. The final section of Act One is the beginning of Cory's own passage into manhood. Though Troy recounted earlier how he rejected his father and that previous life, Troy now embodies his father's previous actions. He goes to attack Cory after Cory angrily returns from the football game, distraught that his coach will not let him play because of Troy's demand that he be kicked off the team. Rose holds Troy back but he verbally attacks his son, using his baseball language. He tells Cory that he now has one strike (of three), and that he shouldn't strike out.

Summary and Analysis of Act II, scene 1

Summary

The next morning, Cory stands by the tree in the yard and tries to hit a baseball with a bat. His swing "is awkward, less sure" than Troy's. Rose enters and Cory tells her that he is not quitting the team. Rose tells him that his father went down to the police station to bail out his uncle Gabe who had gotten into some trouble. Cory goes back into the house just as Troy and Bono come into the yard, complaining about how the police arrest Gabe just so that they can get the fifty dollar bail money that Troy pays to get him out of jail.

Bono begins to help Troy with the fence, but Bono complains that the wood is too hard, that he should have used a soft wood like pine. Troy tells him that this is good outside wood that might last forever. Bono gently chides Troy for having "got tight" with Alberta. Troy resists the chiding and Cory enters and begins to help Bono cut the wood. Cory says that he doesn't know why his mother wants a fence, and Troy echoes this sentiment asking, "What the hell she keeping out with it? She ain't got nothing nobody want." Bono tells them, "Some people build fences to keep people out…and other people build fences to keep people in." Bono explains that Troy has been his guide throughout the years and that he has taken his own pleasure in seeing Troy find happiness in his work and family. He implores Troy to hold on to Rose, saying that he doesn't want to see him mess up.

Troy tells Bono he wasn't intentionally looking for anyone other than Rose but that Alberta "just stuck onto me where I can't shake her loose." He insists he isn't ducking the responsibility of his actions, but that he can't quit being with Alberta either. Bono leaves and Rose enters. Troy informs her of Gabe's troubles and Rose thinks that perhaps putting him in a hospital would be best for him. Troy insists that he wants to see Gabe be free.

Troy tells Rose that he has something to admit to her. He circuitously tries to explain his affair with Alberta and finally tells her he has fathered a child with the woman. Rose is stunned by the news. Gabe enters, holding a rose he tries to give to Rose. Rose asks Troy why he is coming to her with this after eighteen years of marriage. Gabe keeps interrupting their conversation, trying to show off his new quarter and explaining how Troy came and rescued him from the bad men downtown. Rose sends him inside for a piece of watermelon.

Rose tells Troy she might have expected this kind of behavior five or ten years ago but not now. She angrily tells him she has "tried to be everything a wife should be…Been married eighteen years and I got to live to see the day you tell me you been seeing another woman and done fathered a child by her...My whole family is half." Troy tries to be realistic about the situation, telling her there is nothing he can do and that "we can talk this out" but Rose is indignant.

Troy tells Rose that Alberta gives him a different sense of himself, that he "can step out of this house and get away from the pressures and problems...be a different man." Troy says he has been in a pattern, trying to be responsible for his family, and that along the way her forgot about himself. He tries to use baseball analogies to explain his circumstance and that he has fooled the world by bunting when he met her. "I stood on first base for eighteen years and I thought...well, goddamn it...go on for it!" Rose can only tell him he should have stayed in her bed.

Rose tries to explain her own hopes and dreams, how she buried all her feeling in him and held on to him even through her darkest times. She tells Troy he gives to them, but he also takes from them as well. This makes Troy angry and he declares he has given all for his family. Troy grabs Rose and makes threatening gestures. Cory enters the yard from behind and grabs Troy, throwing a glancing blow against his chest. This bold acts stuns both Cory and Troy. Troy starts towards Cory, but Rose holds him back. Troy tells Cory that he now has two strikes on him and that he better not strike out.

Analysis

Cory's awkwardness with the baseball bat is a metaphor for his own feelings of inadequacy in living up to his father's expectations. Though Cory excels in football, his father's swing does not come naturally to him. Wilson visually captures the classic tension between father and son. The son desires to overtake the father and yet in Troy Maxson's life, there is no room for anyone but him.

Bono further elaborates on the play's chief metaphor. In handling the wood for the Maxson's fence, Bono is surprised that Troy didn't get soft pine wood. Troy responds that the hard wood he bought may just last forever. This exchange highlights Troy's own unreasonable feelings of invincibility. He compares his own life to that of the fence he is building, meant to be a symbol for Troy's emotional hardness. Troy's fence becomes not just a barrier to his relationships with his family but also a monument to his failings as a father and husband.

The scene moves into one of the play's most dramatic confrontations. Troy admits to Rose, while she is going about her daily duties as a housewife, that he has been unfaithful to her. It is with some irony that Troy has such a difficult time telling Rose that he is going to be a father since she could question whether he has been much of a father to Cory or Lyons. The tone of the play now becomes angrier and more sorrowful and will remain this way through the second act. Rose cries out to her husband that she tried to be everything for him that a wife should be.

The audience now sees Troy for the truly selfish person that he is. The first act was spent with Troy waxing eloquently, if harshly, on the necessities of responsibility and duty to family. It is clear now that those words were hollow. When Rose tries to reach out to him, Troy only retreats further into himself, claiming that he was with Alberta because she gave him feelings that his family could not give him. Troy is now a man of inconsistency.

It is important to note the choice of language that Troy reverts to after admitting his affair. Troy attempts to explain his actions in the mode of a baseball announcer. This only underscores his self-centeredness, however. Troy creates a game out of his life and places himself as the star player. He uses baseball analogies to try and explain the kind of life that was handed to him versus the kind of life that he desires for himself. The analogies, however, fall flat and Rose is unconvinced. Rose tries to explain to him how his selfishness takes from her and Cory as well, but Troy is not willing to hear this. Troy's anger almost explodes into violence before Cory diverts his rage. He once again uses baseball terminology to threaten Cory but it is Troy who is now the one striking out.

Summary and Analysis of Act II, scenes 2, 3, and 5

Summary

Scene Two

It is six months later. Troy walks out of the house and Rose stops him. He protests that she has not wanted to talk to him for months and now she does. She wants to know if he will be coming home after work tomorrow. He tells her that he is probably going to cash his check, go to the Taylors', and play checkers. Rose exclaims that she cannot live this way. Troy tells Rose that he is going over to the hospital to see Alberta. She is having her baby. Rose tells him that the state authorities went over and took Gabe from Miss Pearl's that afternoon on Troy's orders. Troy says that she is lying by saying that, but Rose says she read it on the papers they submitted to her. "You did Gabe just like you did Cory," she tells him. "You wouldn't sign the paper for Cory...but you signed for Gabe." She tells him that he signed his brother's life away for half his money.

The phone rings and Rose leaves to answer it. She returns a moment later and tells Troy that Alberta has had her baby. Troy is excited and wants to know the gender. Rose tells him that it is a girl and Troy tries to leave to go see her. Then, Rose tells him that Alberta died having the baby. Rose is worried about who will bury her, but Troy is defiant. He enters into "a quiet rage that threatens to consume him." He has a conversation with "Mr. Death" and tells him that he will build a fence around his yard to keep what belongs to him. Death can bring his army, but Troy tells him that he "ain't gonna fall down on my vigilance this time."

Scene Three

Three days later, Rose sits on the porch waiting for Troy to come home in the evening. Troy enters carrying an infant wrapped in blankets and they stand in silence. Troy tells Rose that the baby has no mother, but Rose is indignant. Talking to the baby, but speaking loud enough for Rose to hear, Troy says that he feels no guilt for what he has done because, "it felt right in my heart." He pleads with Rose to take in the baby because she is family and is all he has. Rose concedes and tells Troy, "this child got a mother. But you a womanless man."

Scene Four

Two months later, Lyons comes calling to pay Troy back twenty dollars that he owes him. Rose is preparing to go to church and tells Lyons that Troy will return shortly. Cory enters just as Lyons is leaving and Lyons tells him he is sorry to have missed his graduation. Cory says he is trying to find a job now. Cory goes to the tree and picks up the baseball bat and swings at an imaginary pitch. Troy enters and the two eye each other before Troy goes into the house.

Troy tries to ask Rose where she is going, but she has none of it. Troy begins to sing the old song about his dog Blue and Bono enters. Bono tells Troy he can't keep up with him now that he has his promotion and that he's thinking of retiring in a few years. Troy says he's been thinking the same thing, but Bono can't believe it since Troy has the easier job of driving the truck now. "It's ain't the same, Bono," Troy tells him. "It ain't like working the back of the truck. Ain't got nobody to talk to...fell like you working by yourself. Naw, I'm thinking about retiring." As Bono leaves, Troy remarks that he heard Bono bought his wife a new refrigerator. Bono says he did since Troy kept his end of the bargain and built his fence.

Troy sits on the porch and Cory enters the yard. He tries to get past Troy on the steps, but Troy blocks his way. Cory becomes frustrated and Troy insists that Cory say "excuse me" like a polite person. Troy shoves Cory back as he tries to go by and Cory shouts, "I live here too!" He tells Troy that he isn't scared of him and that "you don't count around here no more." Troy becomes angry and tells Cory that now he is grown and that he should act like it. "...When you get out there in the alley...you can forget about this house. See? Cause this is my house."

Cory angrily retorts that Troy never did anything for him except "try and make me scared of you." He tells him that Rose is scared of him too and this angers Troy even more. Cory dares him to fight. He tells Troy, "You took Uncle Gabe's money he got from the army to buy this house and then you put him out." Troy advances towards Cory and Cory picks up the baseball bat. Troy tells him that he's going to have to use it and kill him if he picks it up and Cory dares him to come at him again. Troy grabs the bat and the two struggle over it. Troy is stronger and takes the bat and stands over him, ready to swing. He stops and tells Cory to leave. Cory says to tell Rose he'll be back for his things and Troy tells him, "They'll be on the other side of that fence." As Cory leaves, Troy assumes a batting posture and again taunts Death.

Analysis

The second scene of Act Two begins six months later. Very quickly the audience is able to see the ways in which Rose and Troy's life has unraveled. She, apparently, has not spoken to him in months. For his part, Troy has made no effort to make amends and has presumably spent his days doing just what he is doing on this day, cashing his check and playing checkers. Troy has also begun to let his other relationships and responsibilities lapse. Rose tells him that Gabe is being taken to a mental hospital and she accuses him of sending him away in order to keep his money. It is a damning accusation.

Rose is then put in the difficult situation of bearing the news of Alberta's death. Her worry about who will bury the woman foreshadows the ways in which Rose takes on Alberta's responsibilities in life, namely raising her daughter. In this turn of events, it is Rose that is shown to be the truly responsible member of the Maxson family.

Wilson's play makes a strongly feminist statement here. While up to this point the audience had only seen Rose as the passive domestic partner, it is clear now that Rose is truly the foundation of the family. This becomes more true as she takes Raynell as her own.

Troy's conversation with "Mr. Death" is a dramatization of his fear of dying. In several instances, most notably his bout with pneumonia, Troy casts himself as narrowly escaping death. For Troy, death is something that is always near to him. Only through his wits is he able to escape it. Alberta's death is a kind of wake-up call for Troy. It is a realization that he has fallen down on his duties as a man and as a human being. Troy's fence now becomes a fence of safety. Instead of keeping his family away from him, his fence is now meant to hold everyone inside.

The next scene, in which Rose takes Raynell as her own daughter, is powerful in expressing both what Troy has gained and lost during the play. Troy has obvious affection for his child. The fact that he has owned his fatherhood and taken in the child shows that he is not completely heartless. However, he is also powerless and can do nothing but ask for Rose's help. Troy's selfishness remains just below the surface during all of this and he cannot help but protest by explaining why he does not apologize.

Troy's infidelity is a symbol of the destruction of the American Dream. Wilson's play is, in effect, a critique of that dream. Though the American Dream has been defined in many different ways, Wilson uses his play to show the audience the ways in which the American Dream has been defined for the African American community by forces outside of that community. Troy's life would seem to be following that dream – he is slowly rising into the middle class, he has a family, and even owns his house which will soon have a picket fence. This dream is an impossibility, however. It is Troy's flaws that destroy this dream. As a universal type of character, Wilson is commenting on the ways that the flaws of humanity make the American Dream an impossibility.

The complete destruction of this dream occurs during Cory and Troy's battle in the front yard. Cory is blunt in forcing Troy to confront his own inadequacies and yet it is Troy who is still the more powerful man. In this scene Troy becomes his father. He kicks Cory out of the house just as his own father kicked him out of his boyhood home. In a cycle, Troy has become the thing that he hated most.

Summary and Analysis of Act II, scene 5

Summary

The final scene is set in 1965, eight years since Corey left home. It is the morning of Troy's funeral. There is little activity outside the house until the door opens and Raynell comes out into the yard. Rose calls for her and tells her to get dressed. She goes to a small garden plot and tells her mother she is checking to see if her garden grew overnight. Rose tells her that she just has to give it a chance. As Raynell continues to poke at her garden with a stick, Cory enters, dressed in a Marine corporal's uniform. "His posture is that of a military man, and his speech has a clipped sternness."

Cory asks Raynell if her mother is home and Rose comes out and tearfully embraces her son. Bono and Lyons come out of the house and marvel at Cory's transformation. Bono tells Cory that he looks like Troy as a young man. Lyons dotes on Raynell and Rose introduces the girl to Cory, the older brother she's never met. Rose tries to feed Cory breakfast, but he refuses.

Lyons and Cory talk for a while. Cory is getting married and Lyons tells him that he and Bonnie split up four years ago, about the time that Troy retired from the sanitation department. Lyons encourages Cory to stay in the military and retire early, that there is "nothing out here" for him in Pittsburgh. He tells Cory that he is in a workhouse right now, punishment for a check cashing scheme he was caught in. He remembers that Troy once told him that "you got to take the crookeds with the straights" and so that's what he reminds himself of. He remembers how he once saw his father strike out three times in a row and then hit a home run right out of Homestead Field. "He wasn't satisfied hitting in the seats...he want to hit it over everything!"

Lyons goes inside to eat breakfast and Raynell comes back out. She asks him if he used to sleep in her room and he says yes. She tells him that Troy always called it "Cory's room" and that some of his football equipment is still in the closet. Rose sends Raynell in and stands on the porch talking to Cory. She shows him the rag, still tied to the tree, that Troy was swinging at with the baseball bat when he fell over and died. "Seem like he swung it and stood there with this grin on his face," she tells him. Cory tells her that he is not going to go to Troy's funeral and Rose refuses to hear it. He tells her that he can't "drag Papa with me everywhere I go. I've got to say no to him." Rose demands that he put his anger aside and that he needs to come to some peace about the whole thing. Cory wants to find a way to get rid of Troy, but Rose tells him that he is just like his father.

She tells him that Troy's shadow in his life was nothing but "you growing into yourself." She tells him, "Your daddy wanted you to be everything he wasn't ...and at the same time he tried to make you into everything he was." Rose tells him that she once thought Troy could fill all the empty spaces in her life as a mother and a wife but that Troy was so big, he filled the whole place up. In order to keep his strength, she had to give up some of hers. Taking in Raynell offered her the chance to once again be a mother, to have "all them babies I had wanted but never had."

Raynell comes back out and asks Cory if he knows about Blue. Raynell tells him that Blue is Troy's old dog he always used to sing about. Together they start singing Troy's song about Blue. The final verse is about Blue's funeral and ends with Blue "treeing possums in the Promised Land."

Cory gets up and stands by the tree. Gabriel enters the yard. Lyons comes out and tells Rose he knew that the hospital would let him out to come to Troy's funeral. Gabe tells Rose that it's time, that he's "gonna tell St. Peter to open the gates." He picks up his old trumpet without a mouthpiece and gets ready to blow. He puts all his effort into blowing into the trumpet "like a man who has been waiting some twenty-odd years for this single moment." As he blows, no sound comes out. Gabe suddenly has a "frightful realization" and is "bare and exposed." He begins a slow strange dance of "atavistic signature and ritual." Gabriel pushes Lyons away and tries to howl a song. "He finishes his dance and the gates of heaven stand open as wide as God's closet." He yells out: "That's the way that go!" and the scene goes black.

Analysis

The final scene of the play can be understood through the same language of baseball that Troy Maxson uses to narrate his own life. In an earlier scene, Troy compared his relationships with Rose, Cory, and Alberta to running the bases on a baseball diamond. It is Troy, however, that the audience now sees has struck out. His first strike came with his unfaithfulness to Rose, the woman who supported and stood by him for half her life. His second strike came when he destroyed his relationship with his son, Cory. It is death that serves as Troy's third and final strike.

It is important to note the setting for this scene. It is 1965, and though Wilson does not allude to it, much change has been made in the racial dynamic of the United States in the eight years that have passed. This setting, in fact, alludes to what is considered the most important Civil Rights legislation of the era – the Voting Rights Act of 1965. Troy's death is a line of demarcation. He represents the passing of a particular era of African American history. His generation led the great migration to the North and sowed the seeds of unrest that resulted in great change. Troy's absence represents an opening of space for a new generation to heal and to grow.

This rite of passage between generations is seen in two powerful scenes in this final act. In the first scene, Cory returns and meets his baby half-sister for the first time. They have nothing in common, no shared experiences or memories, yet are able to together perform the song of Old Blue that Troy taught them. Despite his bitterness and unfaithfulness, the song symbolizes Troy's ability to bequeath something of his own life and himself to his children.

This scene is also an example of the role of the blues in the play. The blues is a uniquely African American musical form. It is music of sin and redemption; the blues chronicles the emotions of a neglected race in America. Troy's story is a blues story. He is the maligned character that the world has turned against. Alberta represents his sin and Rose his chance at redemption - a redemption he fails to claim. Blues provides the play's bitter rhythm and in this final scene Raynell and Cory's song becomes a blues dirge.

The second important action in this scene is Gabriel's entrance to blow the trumpet and let Troy into heaven. Earlier in the play, Gabriel assured Troy that St. Peter had his name written in his book in heaven. This would be his ticket through the pearly gates. Gabriel's trumpet, however, does not emit a sound. Gabriel does not give up and begins a ritual dance. This dance is open to interpretation by the audience, but its power is that it achieves Troy's redemption. The gates of heaven are opened. Gabriel, thus, is the play's redeeming figure. He represents the victory of innocence and family bonds. He does not give up on Troy even while his wife and son are ready to be done with the man. Troy becomes the redeemed, though deeply flawed, hero.

Suggested Essay Questions

1. **Why does Gabriel carry a trumpet around his neck?**

   Because of a head injury, Gabriel believes that he is the angel Gabriel and that he is able to open the gates of heaven with his trumpet. While the audience knows that this is not literally true, the final scene shows that Gabe becomes the play's figure of redemption. He unsuccessfully tries to blow his trumpet and when that does not work, dances his brother into heaven. Troy does not have the play's last word; instead, it is the fool, the representation of innocence, that finally offers Troy deliverance.
2. **Why is the setting of the play important?**

   The setting of the play is important because the 1950's represents a time of great upheaval in race relations in the United States. Troy Maxson represents a previous generation that now watches the world move on around them. They have been maligned by white transgression in the past and yet have been able to procure a small portion of the country's booming wealth for themselves. Troy dies, however, in 1965, the year of the greatest legislative triumph of the Civil Rights era. He is not able to enjoy the victory that he helped bring about.
3. **Why is Troy Maxson considered an "everyman" character?**

   Troy Maxson is a character of universal type. Though his life is dictated by the particulars of the African American experience of the early twentieth century, his failings as a man as well as his small measures of redemption are applicable to all people. Wilson deftly creates a character who is a flawed and identifiable hero, through his responsibilities to family and his inabilities to live up to his own high expectations. His battles with his sons resonate across racial and cultural lines as universal human experiences.
4. **Explain the play's principal metaphor of the fence.**

   Jim Bono best sums up the play's overarching metaphor by explaining to Troy, "Some people build fences to keep people out...and other people build fences to keep people in." Both Troy and Rose Maxson attempt to build emotional fences throughout the play. Rose attempts to keep her family within her fence by being a good and faithful wife. Troy is more concerned with an emotional fence that never permits his sons to understand his love for them.
5. **Is Rose's character an example of feminism or an example of the repressed role of women in society?**

   Scholars have been divided on Rose's role in the play. Some have seen Rose as the prototypical 1950s housewife, disappearing into her husband and leaving no room for her own self to flourish. Others, however, have seen

Rose as occupying a feminist position; she does remain a housewife and mother but only because she makes the choice for herself. No one forces motherhood on her. She admits that when Troy takes pieces of her, it is because she gives those pieces out of her own choice. But then, what other choice does she have?

6. **Discuss the role of the blues in *Fences*.**

   Troy's blues song for his dog, Old Blue, is an example of Wilson's use of blues music in the play. Troy takes on the role of an archetypal blues character who has seen his world taken away from him for his transgressions. The blues also acts as a form of aural tradition. Cory and Raynell sing Troy's blues song as they bury him, representing pieces of Troy that pass down through generations.

7. **Discuss the meaning of baseball in the play.**

   Troy uses baseball as a metaphor for his own life, yet the audience comes to understand that the game Troy plays is not necessarily the one in which he sees himself. Troy remembers himself as a star in the Negro Leagues, but he was never given a chance to prove himself. His relationship with Alberta, and the selfishness that it inculcates in him, is his chance to please himself in a way that he never could while playing baseball. Troy, however, fails at his own game. His failures in his relationships with his wife and son represent two strikes in his life. The inevitability of his death is his third and final strike.

8. **What traits make Troy Maxson an unlikable protagonist?**

   Troy is seen as an unsympathetic character for much of the play because of the emotional fence he builds to keep his sons and wife from seeing and accepting his underlying love for them. This is best observed when Cory asks Troy why Troy does not like him. Instead of offering a reassuring remark, Troy shames his son by telling him that there is no law that says he must like him. The fence that Troy puts up to keep his sons from accepting him also acts as a fence to keep the audience from sympathizing with Troy.

9. **What traits make Troy Maxson a redeemed protagonist?**

   For all of his faults, Troy Maxson is ultimately redeemed. This is accomplished through the small glimpses of care and affection that his children remember in the play's final scene. Raynell tells Cory that Troy always called her room "Cory's room" and that he never threw out Cory's football equipment. They close the play by singing Troy's old blues song about his dog. It is inevitable that fathers pass on pieces of themselves to their children. Through this process, Troy becomes a redeemed character and a flawed hero, but a hero nevertheless.

10. **Discuss the cycle of father-son relationships in the play.**

In the play, sons become outraged at the actions of their fathers. This outrage turns into hate, and yet the sons cannot help but bear a resemblance to their fathers. For Troy, this happens when he assaults Cory and kicks him out of the house. Troy believes that he is protecting Cory from a life of failure in football, yet Troy has become the same man that his father had been. The final scene sees Cory struggling with this same dynamic. He seeks to reject his father, but he cannot completely leave Troy - he carries his memory, influence, and song with him.

Suggested Essay Questions

Fences and the Negro Leagues

In August Wilson's *Fences*, Troy Maxson is a former Negro League baseball player who narrowly missed the opportunity to play in the Major Leagues. When he was a young player at the top of his game, Major League Baseball was segregated. The first African American baseball players were not recruited to the majors until Troy was already too old to be a viable team member. This experience leaves Troy cold and bitter, and it influences his relationship with his son, Cory, who has aspirations of playing college football.

This experience was not an uncommon one for the scores of African American ball players who played in the Negro Leagues. Only now, approximately fifty years after the dissolution of the last Negro League teams, are the skills and talent of these Negro League players beginning to be honored by modern day baseball. A look at the history of Negro League baseball offers a glimpse into a world of segregation, but it also offers a look at an elite group of skilled players representing their communities on a national stage.

Until the 1950's, baseball in America mirrored the broader racial culture. In baseball, the all-white National and American Leagues garnered most of the money, prestige, and attention for professional sports fans. African American ballplayers played in the Negro Leagues. The Negro Leagues had their beginnings in the late nineteenth and early twentieth centuries with the organization of the first professional, paid teams of baseball players. These teams would participate in circuits, called Barnstormer leagues, where teams would travel across the United States playing in large cities and small towns or anywhere else that provided a field and fans. In 1920 the first professional league of black baseball teams was organized by Rube Foster, a baseball pitcher and manager. The league was named the Negro National League. It consisted of eight team: the Chicago American Giants, Chicago Giants, Dayton Marcos, Detroit Stars, Indianapolis ABC's, Kansas City Monarchs, St. Louis Giants, and the Cuban Stars.

The history of Negro league baseball is best seen through the careers of famous Negro legends Satchel Paige and Josh Gibson (both are mentioned in Wilson's play). Paige is considered to be not just one of the best Negro league pitchers ever but also one of the greatest pitchers in the history of the entire game of baseball. Paige notoriously refused to give his exact age, though historians of the game have determined that he was born sometime around 1906-1908 in Mobile, Alabama. Paige suffered a rough childhood – he was born into poverty and resorted to stealing by the time he was a boy. He was sent to Mt. Meigs Juvenile detention center as a child. It was here that Paige first learned the game of baseball and learned that he had a special talent for pitching.

Paige played for at least eight Negro league baseball teams throughout his career, though his time spent in the Barnstorming leagues and in South American winter leagues meant that his career was much more prolific than what can be verified. Because statistics were not widely kept during Paige's career, his legacy has relied more on legend than on numbers. Paige would famously call in his outfielders or tell his infielders to sit down when he was pitching to certain batters, so sure was he of his ability to strike the batter out. In the Negro league World Series of 1942, Paige claimed that he intentionally loaded the bases just so that he could pitch to Josh Gibson, the league's best batter, and strike him out on three straight pitches.

Gibson himself is, perhaps, a model for Troy Maxson in Wilson' play. Gibson was known as the best hitter in Negro league baseball. According to the Baseball Hall of Fame, into which Gibson was inducted in 1972, Gibson hit almost 800 home runs in his career (the current leader in career homes runs is Barry Bond with 762). While this number is impossible to validate since, like Paige, Gibson's statistics were never officially kept by league officials, these stories of legendary ability speak to the status that such players held in the imaginations of fans and baseball historians.

Like Troy Maxson in *Fences*, Josh Gibson would never play in the white Major Leagues. This fact haunted Gibson for much of his life. Later in his life, he is reported to have suffered from alcoholism and depression, diseases that his former teammates and friends say was brought on by his frustration and disappointment with the game. Gibson died of a stroke in 1947, just months before baseball was integrated when Jackie Robinson signed a contract with the Brooklyn Dodgers.

Satchel Paige, on the other hand, would get the chance to play in the Major Leagues. At the age of 42, Paige was signed by the Cleveland Indians to pitch from their bullpen during the pennant race of 1948. Though his pitching was not as electric as it had been in his younger days, Paige played a crucial role in helping the Indians win the American League pennant that year. In 1965, in what was considered a gimmick promotion, Paige was brought on to pitch in a game for the Kansas City Royals. He thus became the oldest man to ever pitch or play in the Major Leagues.

The Negro leagues, as seen through the lives of its players, is remembered as a symbol of both great injustice and great achievement. Several of its players, including Jackie Robinson and Hank Aaron, would go on to legendary careers in the Major Leagues. Most of the league's great players, however, were denied the chance to compete against their white counterparts. Players such as Gibson and Paige, including other great stars like Monte Irvin, Cool Papa Bell, and Judy Johnson, are remembered for their individual achievements but also for the way they ushered in a golden era of black baseball. Through such players, baseball was not just white America's game. It was a game for all.

Author of ClassicNote and Sources

Lane Davis, author of ClassicNote. Completed on November 27, 2010, copyright held by GradeSaver.

Updated and revised Elizabeth Weinbloom January 10, 2011. Copyright held by GradeSaver.

August Wilson. Fences. New York: Plume, 1986.

Ladrica Menson-Furr. August Wilson's Fences. New York: Continuum Internation Publishing Group, 2008.

Sandra G. Shannon. August Wilson's Fences: A Reference Guide. Westport, CT: Greenwood Publishing Group, 2003.

Alan Nadel. May All Your Fences Have Gates: Essays on the Drama of August Wilson. Iowa City: University of Iowa Press, 1994.

"Negro Leagues Baseball Players Association." 2010-11-10. <http://www.nlbpa.com/history.html>.

"Negro League History 101." Negro League Baseball. 2010-11-11. <http://www.negroleaguebaseball.com/history101.html>.

Essay: The Importance of Dreams

by Laura Lee
February 15, 2003

Throughout the history of black American culture, the pursuit of dreams has played a pivotal role in self-fulfillment and internal development. In many ways an individual's reactions to the perceived and real obstacles barring the path to a dream define the very character of that person. This theme has been quite evident in black literary works regardless of time period or writing style. For example, in both Fences, by August Wilson, and Their Eyes Were Watching God, by Zora Neale Hurston, dreams enhance the plot and message of the story, though the two stories develop under different circumstances. The importance of dreams in character development is one common thread that unites Fences and Their Eyes Were Watching God, two stories penned by authors similar only in their racial backgrounds.

While Their Eyes Were Watching God focuses little on the dreams of men, the author's attitude toward this subject is clear from the very first paragraph of her novel. She claims that men's dreams are "mocked to death by Time", implying that men are so inherently passive that they have less control than the "tide" over their own desires (Hurston 1). Logan Killicks and Joe Starks provide physical representations of this opinion. Logan's dream seems to be to find a beautiful woman to love. While his marriage to Janie fulfills this wish, the reader witnesses Logan's inability to hold on to Janie; Janie soon leaves Logan with no control and little hope. Joe, too, fails to succeed, but he is shiftless in another way. While he perseveres in accomplishing his dreams, he spends his life pursuing the wrong dreams. Janie accuses him of not seeing or understanding a "whole heap uh things" he "could have"; how true it is! (Hurston 86) Rather than accepting the facts of life and making plans around them, Joe unrealistically expected everyone and everything to conform to his desires. Tea Cake is the one male who does accomplish his dreams. However, his unique personality explains his success. Tea Cake has priorities and knows exactly what will make him truly happy, and he does not give up on his dreams, no matter how unrealistic they may seem. Even though he "ain't got no business" getting "familiar"(Hurston 105) with Janie, he comes back "day after day" (Hurston 111) because he realizes that Janie will make him happy. Hurston's observations of the actions of the male characters in Their Eyes Were Watching God provides crucial commentary on how different characters react to adversity.

In Fences, as well, the reader understands Wilson's view that weak characters, usually men, will allow excuses and roadblocks to interfere in the attainment of their dreams. Troy best typifies the kind of behavior that succumbs to bitterness and inaction rather than persisting in a dream. His defeatist attitude shows in his relations with his son; he tells his son that football "ain't gonna get" him "nowhere" (Wilson 8). Because Troy's dream to play professional baseball never materialized, he tells

Cory to learn something that "can't nobody take away" (Wilson 35). However, Troy's life revolves around baseball; while he may not have played professional ball, it is clear that baseball gave him something priceless. Still, Troy is so upset about his failed dreams that he blames all his failures on others and becomes one-dimensionally focused on tangible goals. He drives those who love him away. In the other male characters of the play the same trends of hopelessness and lack of effort are evident. Wilson clearly demonstrates the self-inflicted pain that Troy and others suffer as a result of the frustrations of their desires.

In Their Eyes Were Watching God Hurston provides the antithesis of this male weakness through the strong perseverance of Janie in fulfilling her dreams. At the beginning of her novel, Hurston comments that the "dream is the truth"; women "act...accordingly" (Hurston 1). This contrasts greatly with her indictment of the condition of man. The reader witnesses throughout the novel Janie's great internal strength as well as her flexibility in accomplishing her goal of finding true love. While she certainly meets failure in the shape of Logan and Jody, she eventually does find happiness because of her resilience. Through two failed marriages she still manages to hold on to her ideal of the "blossoming pear tree" (Hurston 11). Her dreams may have changed in form, but remained the same in substance; as she put it, her "old thoughts" simply needed "new words"(Hurston 32). Joe died too proud to acknowledge his mistakes, but Janie made her horrible experiences little more than a "sobbing sigh" (Hurston 192) due to her endless search and eventual discovery of "peace" (Hurston 193). Janie displays enviable qualities of optimism, a sense of self-worth, and dedication in the pursuit of her dreams.

August Wilson also counters his weak male characters in Fences with the strong female presence of Rose. Rose's dreams center around a hope for a stable, loving family, something that she lacked as a child. Rose sacrifices everything to "hold on" to her family because she realizes how important her strength is to the rest of the family (Wilson 61). She even mothers the child that Troy has with another woman because she knows how much that child will need love. Rose denies herself of her "wants and needs" because her ultimate dream is to build a foundation and a future; she recognizes that this is the most important priority in her life (Wilson 71). While her path is not always easy, Rose sticks to it because she knows exactly who she is and what she wants. She does not condone Troy's actions, even warning him that he is "livin' on borrowed time", but she recognizes that his mistakes should not ruin her dream. Rose shows traits of motivation and adaptability that allow her to accomplish her dream in spite of her circumstances.

In both Their Eyes Were Watching God and Fences references to dreams continually appear. It seems logical that the concept of dreams and their attainability would be frequently addressed in writings of black American authors; after all, blacks have always encountered numerous difficulties in accomplishing anything that whites would never face. In Fences especially racial barriers play a great role in the impossibility of dreams; however, Fences also demonstrates that how an individual reacts to adversity can greatly influence his or her life. Their Eyes Were Watching

God provides a more universal analysis of whether dreams can be achieved; Janie faces less barriers because of her race than she does because of the people surrounding her. An interesting aspect of Fences and Their Eyes Were Watching God is that the women do display much greater hope and dedication than do the men. One possible argument for this could be that women have historically played a subordinate role to men while also having more responsibilities; because of this, women are forced to ignore many hardships and continue in their dreams while men can simply give up. Regardless of this, it is fascinating to observe how many parallels there are between Fences and Their Eyes Were Watching God regarding dreams. The two books little resemble each other on a purely literal level because Wilson and Hurston use such unique writing styles; however, the message and opinions of the two are remarkably similar.

The crucial importance of dreams in one's life plays a key role in both Their Eyes Were Watching God, by Zora Neale Hurston, and Fences, by August Wilson. The two stories, differing in characterization, setting, and plot, have similar themes of the necessity of discovering one's true desires and living by the standards of those dreams. Zora Neale Hurston and August Wilson are continually recognized simply as "black authors"; perhaps these similarities in content will lend some meaning to the term.

Essay: The Significance of Songs in August Wilson's Fences

by Auvijit Chakder
February 29, 2004

"Some people build fences to keep people out, and other people build fences to keep people in," offers the sage Bono one afternoon during his usual bonhomie with fellow refuse collector Troy Maxson. The seemingly minor line encompasses the entire leitmotif of August Wilson's play, Fences. It is a play that takes place in a time, as the author says, that is "turbulent, racing, dangerous, and provocative" and during which the collective fences of society begin to dissolve. It is a time that will leave many, like Troy, confused about the changing nature of family and country. Wilson utilizes song to reveal the nature of the emotional and physical fences, which serve to plague or protect the characters in Fences. The songs, which permeate the lives of the Maxsons, reveal how Troy imposes his fences on his wife and children, and how these characters react to such fences.

Wilson's use of song reveals much about the characters and their relationships with one another. "Jesus be a fence all around me everyday," sings Rose one morning while hanging up the laundry. She sings to be "protected as [she] travels on [her] way." As the first instance of song in the play, this song helps to reveal Rose's mentality regarding her role as wife and mother. Rose asks her husband Troy to build a physical fence around their yard. Bono, a family friend, sees this as a means of "holding on" to Troy because "she loves [him]." This woman has "eighteen years of [her] life invested in Troy" with no other means of keeping Troy faithful but to pray, as with this song. Yet her efforts are abortive as Troy not only cheats on her, but announces that he is "gonna be someone's daddy." At this point in their marriage, Troy and Rose had "lost touch with one another," but she takes the child into her family, and raises her for the reason that "you can't visit the sins of the father upon the child." She deems Troy "a womanless man," however, for straying from her protective fence while she has remained obediently within his.

Song appears later in the play when Troy revisits the music of his father, whose song reveals Troy's mentality regarding his family. Admonished by Rose for calling her as if she were a dog, he starts singing his father's song about "a dog [whose] name was Blue." Troy then reflects on a dog he had once who "used to get uppity like that [ie. like Rose had done]" and would not come when he called. The nature of the song reflects Troy's attitude towards his family on whom he imposes figurative fences. He expects his family to obey his word, as if they were dogs themselves, and builds restrictive fences to keep them as helpless under his dominion as dogs. He builds fences around Rose to keep her "settled down to cook his supper and clean his sheets", and another around Cory to keep him from "getting involved in any sports." He builds yet another to separate himself from Lyons, whose views of life and purpose differ greatly from Troy's own. Rose "took on his life as [hers]" and he prevented Cory from playing football. Rose later reflects that "he was so big he filled up the whole house;" perhaps this is the secret behind why his fences succeeded and why hers did not. Troy had the power to uphold his fences by brute force or by overpowering the entire family. Rose had let him dominate, and was left with no room for her own fence.

Wilson concludes the play with more song, revealing what happens to a fence once it's owner dies. After Troy's death, it is his own song that unites his children. Cory and Raynell, born of different mothers but both blood descendents of Troy. "Had an old dog his name was Blue," sing the two children. Both had learned it from their father, and as their duet comes to an end, one gets the sense of closure. The song is an example of all that Cory shares with his father, including much of his personality. "You're Troy Maxson all over again," says Rose to her song. Cory realizes how much of his father has become part of him and decides to attend his funeral after lingering doubts about acknowledging his father's place in his heart. The "shadow" that was Troy Maxson has become Cory "growing into himself," as Rose puts it. Furthermore, both he and Raynell bond in this moment through their father's song. This song is something they both have in common, and it gives Troy one last chance to unite his children, even though it occurs after his death. It is one last fence to keep his family within.

In Fences, Wilson makes use of song to reveal the fences the characters build around them and those they love. The play takes place in a time when the fences built to keep African-Americans from fulfilling their dreams were just being lifted. The songs reveal the mentality of the Maxsons in response to the changing times and to the barriers they perceive between themselves and their family members. They are songs that have the capacity to restrict, ostracize, and ultimately build the fences that tie families together.

Quiz 1

1. **In what city is "Fences" set?**
   A. Newark
   B. Philadelphia
   C. New York
   D. Pittsburg

2. **By whom is Troy Maxson employed?**
   A. the sanitation department
   B. the paper mill
   C. the water works
   D. the sewage company

3. **How old is Troy?**
   A. 35
   B. 47
   C. 53
   D. 67

4. **On what day of the week is Troy paid?**
   A. Friday
   B. Saturday
   C. Thursday
   D. Wednesday

5. **Over what issue is Troy fighting his superiors at his job?**
   A. the weight of the trash cans
   B. the inability of workers to unionize
   C. the length of the work day
   D. driving the garbage truck

6. **In what decade is "Fences" set?**
   A. 1940's
   B. 1950's
   C. 1960's
   D. 1970's

7. **What state is Alberta from?**
   A. Alabama
   B. Georgia
   C. Florida
   D. Mississippi

8. **What grocery store does Rose prefer to shop at?**
   A. Safeway
   B. Morrison's
   C. the A&P
   D. Bella's

9. **What sickness did Troy have that almost killed him in 1941?**
   A. tuberculosis
   B. whooping cough
   C. pneumonia
   D. sleeping sickness

10. **How much money does Lyons want to borrow from his father?**
    A. $5
    B. $10
    C. $15
    D. $100

11. **What is Lyons' girlfriend's name?**
    A. Bonnie
    B. Connie
    C. Alberta
    D. Sarah

12. **According to the Troy, what business is the devil in when he knocks on Troy's door?**
    A. gambling
    B. furniture sales
    C. television sales
    D. sanitation

13. **How much money does Troy say he sends the devil each month?**
   A. $5
   B. $10
   C. $15
   D. $100

14. **Where does Bono work?**
   A. the sanitation department
   B. the paper mill
   C. the water works
   D. the sewage company

15. **In her song, who does Rose ask "to protect me as I travel on my way?"**
   A. Love
   B. Troy
   C. Jesus
   D. Mr. President

16. **What remedy does Rose prescribe for Troy's grumblings in the second scene of Act One.**
   A. coffee
   B. time by himself
   C. gin
   D. sex

17. **What kind of business did Pope start with his lottery winnings?**
   A. a textile mill
   B. a garbage collection service
   C. a fence building service
   D. a restaurant

18. **Where does Cory go when he goes out in the second scene of Act One?**
   A. school
   B. the local hangout
   C. the A&P
   D. football practice

19. **In which war did Gabriel fight in?**
   A. World War I
   B. Korean War
   C. World War II
   D. Vietnam War

20. **What kind of injury did Gabriel sustain as a soldier?**
   A. leg wound
   B. head wound
   C. emotional wounds
   D. loss of limb

21. **What does Gabriel sell around town?**
   A. liquor
   B. cans
   C. sheet metal
   D. fruit

22. **Who does Gabriel mistakenly believe he is?**
   A. Peter Gabriel
   B. God
   C. The angel Gabriel
   D. a hellhound

23. **According to Gabe, who has Troy's name in his book?**
   A. St. Peter
   B. God
   C. Jesus
   D. the preacher

24. **What kind of instrument does Gabe wear around his neck?**
   A. a flute
   B. a basoon
   C. a trumpet
   D. a tuba

25. **How much money does Gabe receive from the government after his war injury?**

A. five hundred dollars
B. two thousand dollars
C. three thousand dollars
D. fifteen hundred dollars

Quiz 1 Answer Key

1. (**D**) Pittsburg
2. (**A**) the sanitation department
3. (**C**) 53
4. (**A**) Friday
5. (**D**) driving the garbage truck
6. (**B**) 1950's
7. (**C**) Florida
8. (**C**) the A&P
9. (**C**) pneumonia
10. (**B**) $10
11. (**A**) Bonnie
12. (**B**) furniture sales
13. (**B**) $10
14. (**A**) the sanitation department
15. (**C**) Jesus
16. (**A**) coffee
17. (**D**) a restaurant
18. (**D**) football practice
19. (**C**) World War II
20. (**B**) head wound
21. (**D**) fruit
22. (**C**) The angel Gabriel
23. (**A**) St. Peter
24. (**C**) a trumpet
25. (**C**) three thousand dollars

Quiz 2

1. **What did Troy buy with Gabe's disability money?**
   A. a house
   B. furniture
   C. a car
   D. an education

2. **Where does Troy go to listen to the ball game?**
   A. the bar
   B. the Smiths'
   C. the Taylors'
   D. Bono's

3. **Who does Gabe live with?**
   A. Miss Pearl
   B. Miss Smith
   C. Miss Taylor
   D. Miss Alberta

4. **What sport does Cory play?**
   A. hockey
   B. baseball
   C. football
   D. basketball

5. **In what year was "Fences" first performed?**
   A. 1966
   B. 1973
   C. 1985
   D. 2001

6. **What does Cory forget to do before heading out to football practice in the second scene of Act One?**
   A. build the fence
   B. shop for the groceries
   C. his chores
   D. walk the dog

7. **What appliance does Cory want Troy to buy?**
    A. a stove
    B. a TV
    C. a dishwasher
    D. a mircrowave

8. **According to Cory, how much does it cost to buy a TV?**
    A. one hundred dollars
    B. two hundred dollars
    C. four hundred dollars
    D. three hundred dollars

9. **Instead of a TV, what does Troy say he will buy?**
    A. a fence
    B. a heater
    C. a car
    D. a roof

10. **Why doesn't Troy want to listen to the Pittsburgh Pirate's games?**
    A. they rejected Troy as a yound ball player
    B. they are not very good
    C. Troy doesn't like baseball
    D. they have an all white team

11. **How much does Cory have to save before Troy will help him buy a TV?**
    A. one hundred dollars
    B. two hundred dollars
    C. four hundred dollars
    D. three hundred dollars

12. **What is the name of the "Puerto Rican boy" on the Pittsburgh Pirates?**
    A. Bordem
    B. Clemente
    C. Gonzalez
    D. Reyes

13. **What famous Negro League pitcher does Troy claim to have hit seven home runs off of?**
    A. Hank Aaron
    B. Josh Gibson
    C. Warren Spahn
    D. Satchel Paige

14. **What is the name of Cory's boss at the A&P?**
    A. Mr. Smith
    B. Mr. Chadwick
    C. Mr. Stawicki
    D. Mr. Bono

15. **Instead of football, what does Troy want Cory to do?**
    A. pick up a trade
    B. stay home and care for his mother
    C. go to college
    D. play jazz like his brother

16. **What title does Troy violently demand that Cory call him?**
    A. father
    B. captain
    C. Mr.
    D. sir

17. **Troy reasons that if he is mean to Cory, Cory will do what?**
    A. will need to borrow money from him
    B. move away from his life
    C. finally know his father is a great man
    D. only love him more

18. **What does the TV set discussed in Act One, Scene Three symbolize?**
    A. the pace of modernity
    B. the American Dream
    C. consumer culture
    D. all of these

19. **When Cory picks up the phone in Act One, scene four, what does he discuss with his friend?**
    A. football plays
    B. college scholarships
    C. football spikes
    D. girls

20. **What is the name of Troy's boss at the sanitation department?**
    A. Mr. Smith
    B. Mr. Ron
    C. Mr. Rand
    D. Mr. Paul

21. **What is Troy's lone historical significance?**
    A. the first man to be called up to the major leagues
    B. the first black man to come before the union
    C. the first black garbage truck driver
    D. the first man to own a house in the Hill District

22. **Why is Troy concerned with Sefus' club being raided by the police?**
    A. because Troy goes there sometimes
    B. because no one likes the cops
    C. because Lyons works there
    D. because it means more people will be out of jobs

23. **What is the name of Troy's old dead dog?**
    A. Old Blue
    B. Old Pink
    C. Old Yeller
    D. Old Red

24. **What kind of flower does Gabriel always bring to Rose?**
    A. a daisey
    B. a petunia
    C. a fern
    D. a rose

25. **What name does Troy use to describe jazz music?**

A. Chinese music

B. rattle and roll music

C. beatdown music

D. dirty music

Quiz 2 Answer Key

1. (**A**) a house
2. (**C**) the Taylors'
3. (**A**) Miss Pearl
4. (**C**) football
5. (**C**) 1985
6. (**C**) his chores
7. (**B**) a TV
8. (**B**) two hundred dollars
9. (**D**) a roof
10. (**D**) they have an all white team
11. (**A**) one hundred dollars
12. (**B**) Clemente
13. (**D**) Satchel Paige
14. (**C**) Mr. Stawicki
15. (**A**) pick up a trade
16. (**D**) sir
17. (**B**) move away from his life
18. (**D**) all of these
19. (**C**) football spikes
20. (**C**) Mr. Rand
21. (**C**) the first black garbage truck driver
22. (**C**) because Lyons works there
23. (**A**) Old Blue
24. (**D**) a rose
25. (**A**) Chinese music

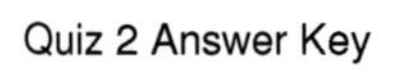
Quiz 2 Answer Key

Quiz 3

1. **According to Bono, what had his father been searching for during his travels?**
   A. the right woman
   B. a place to raise a family
   C. a message from God
   D. the "New Land"

2. **How many children did Troy's father raise?**
   A. eleven
   B. eighteen
   C. ten
   D. four

3. **What two things did Troy's father always make sure his children had?**
   A. food and a roof
   B. a home and a future
   C. a roof and clothes
   D. food and education

4. **When he was fourteen, whose daughter did Troy go "sniffing around?"**
   A. Miles Stawicki
   B. Max Lager
   C. Joe Canewell
   D. Jim Kingwood

5. **After Troy's father beats him, what does Troy do?**
   A. he leaves home
   B. he burns down his father's house
   C. he returns to work
   D. he kills his father

6. **What happened to Troy in Pittsburgh when he tried to rob a man?**
   A. Troy slyly talked his way out of trouble
   B. he was shot and he killed a man
   C. he shot a man with a knife
   D. the man was a cop and arrested him

7. **After he leaves home, what city does Troy first go to?**
   A. Mobile
   B. Atlanta
   C. New Orleans
   D. Pittsburgh

8. **How long was Troy in prison?**
   A. fifteen years
   B. ten years
   C. four years
   D. twenty five years

9. **Troy tells only one character directly that he loves them. Who is it?**
   A. Gabe
   B. Bono
   C. Rose
   D. Cory

10. **In what year was August Wilson born?**
   A. 1933
   B. 1945
   C. 1955
   D. 1963

11. **At what age did Troy leave his home?**
   A. fifteen
   B. fourteen
   C. twenty one
   D. twenty four

12. **Who did Troy go to and tell that Cory couldn't play football?**
   A. the principal
   B. the recruiter
   C. his coach
   D. Mr. Stawicki

13. **Who does Troy have to bail out of jail?**
    A. Alberta
    B. Gabe
    C. Bono
    D. Cory

14. **How much does Troy have to pay the police for bail money?**
    A. fifty dollars
    B. sixty dollars
    C. eighty dollars
    D. seventy dollars

15. **Who tells Troy that some people build fences "to keep people in...."**
    A. Bono
    B. Rose
    C. Cory
    D. Mr. Stawicki

16. **Who does Bono say has been his "guide" in life?**
    A. Gabe
    B. Cory
    C. Troy
    D. Lyons

17. **According to Troy, what kind of music is "Chinese" music?**
    A. classical
    B. jazz
    C. blues
    D. rock and roll

18. **Who got "stuck" onto Troy?**
    A. Alberta
    B. Bono
    C. Rose
    D. Cory

19. **When Gabe interupts their serious conversation over Tory's affiar, what kind of food does Rose send Gabe into the house for?**
    A. pigsfeet
    B. biscuits
    C. watermelon
    D. grits

20. **August Wilson wrote a series of ten plays all set in what city?**
    A. Newark
    B. Philadelphia
    C. New York
    D. Pittsburgh

21. **What kind of analogies does Troy use to describe his relationship with Alberta?**
    A. trash collection analogies
    B. television analogies
    C. baseball analogies
    D. football analogies

22. **During their first physical fight, where does Cory hit Troy?**
    A. in the arm
    B. in the face
    C. in the ribs
    D. in the chest

23. **Who is considered to be the greatest pitcher of the Negro Leagues?**
    A. Jackie Robinson
    B. Josh Gibson
    C. Troy Maxson
    D. Satchel Paige

24. **Whose house does Troy always go to play checkers?**
    A. the Stawicki's
    B. the Bono's
    C. the Smith's
    D. the Taylor's

25. **With whom does Gabe live?**

A. Miss Bono
B. Miss Pearl
C. Miss Smith
D. Miss Culbert

Quiz 3 Answer Key

1. **(D)** the "New Land"
2. **(A)** eleven
3. **(A)** food and a roof
4. **(C)** Joe Canewell
5. **(A)** he leaves home
6. **(B)** he was shot and he killed a man
7. **(A)** Mobile
8. **(A)** fifteen years
9. **(B)** Bono
10. **(B)** 1945
11. **(B)** fourteen
12. **(C)** his coach
13. **(B)** Gabe
14. **(A)** fifty dollars
15. **(A)** Bono
16. **(C)** Troy
17. **(B)** jazz
18. **(A)** Alberta
19. **(C)** watermelon
20. **(D)** Pittsburgh
21. **(C)** baseball analogies
22. **(D)** in the chest
23. **(D)** Satchel Paige
24. **(D)** the Taylor's
25. **(B)** Miss Pearl

Quiz 4

1. **In what year was Major League baseball integrated?**
   A. 1907
   B. 1947
   C. 1950
   D. 1972

2. **How does Alberta die?**
   A. in childbirth
   B. in a car accident
   C. in a kitchen fire
   D. from a stroke

3. **With whom is Troy always having conversations of "quiet rage?"**
   A. Mr. Death
   B. Alberta
   C. Rose
   D. Cory

4. **Three days after Alberta's death, who does Troy bring home with him?**
   A. Alberta's body
   B. his son
   C. Bono
   D. his daughter

5. **What reason does Troy give for not apologizing for his affair?**
   A. "You never cared for me"
   B. "I was only doing what felt good"
   C. "I can do what I want"
   D. "it felt right in my heart"

6. **What does Troy lose when he brings home his daughter?**
   A. his authority
   B. his woman
   C. his friendships
   D. his dignity

7. **Eventually, who takes in Troy's daughter?**
   A. Mr. and Mrs. Bono
   B. Lyons and Bonnie
   C. Alberta's family
   D. Rose

8. **What important event in Cory's life did Lyons miss?**
   A. his graduation
   B. his last football game
   C. his scholarship signing
   D. his military enlistment

9. **What hangs on the tree in the yard and acts as a baseball target?**
   A. a rag
   B. a ball
   C. a tire
   D. a rope

10. **What kind of music does Troy sing throughout the play?**
   A. rock
   B. jazz
   C. blues
   D. swing

11. **What insult does Cory throw at Troy in the fourth scene of Act II?**
   A. "you don't like me"
   B. "you can't have a happy life"
   C. "you are unfaithful"
   D. "you don't count here"

12. **Who would be considered the hero of the play?**
   A. Gabe
   B. Rose
   C. Cory
   D. Troy

13. **According to Cory, what is the only thing Troy ever did for him?**
    A. give him a roof
    B. make him scared
    C. make him cold and uncaring
    D. give him food

14. **What object do Cory and Troy wrestle over?**
    A. a baseball bat
    B. football spikes
    C. a football
    D. a tennis ball

15. **Where does Troy say he will put Cory's stuff after he puts him out?**
    A. under the tree
    B. on the other side of the fence
    C. in the front yard
    D. on the front porch

16. **How many strikes does a batter in baseball get before they strike out?**
    A. two
    B. nine
    C. four
    D. three

17. **How many years pass between Cory's expulsion and Troy's death?**
    A. nine
    B. four
    C. eight
    D. seven

18. **In what year was "Fences" first published?**
    A. 1945
    B. 1972
    C. 1986
    D. 1999

19. **What kind of traditional dramatic device does Gabe serve to portray in the play?**
A. a protagonist
B. a chorus
C. an oracle
D. a villain

20. **Why does Gabe's trumpet not blow in the final scene?**
A. it has no mouthpiece
B. it has no valve
C. he does not know how to play it
D. it is a toy trumpet

21. **What is Gabe intent on opening with his trumpet?**
A. the Holy Bible
B. the gates of hell
C. the gates of heaven
D. the door to enlightenment

22. **In what year is the final scene set?**
A. 1945
B. 1965
C. 1972
D. 1986

23. **What does Raynell check on in the yard before Troy's funeral?**
A. her swingset
B. the tree
C. the garden
D. her ant farm

24. **What branch of the military does Cory enter?**
A. the Army
B. the Navy
C. the Marines
D. the Air Force

25. **What happens to Lyons and Bonnie?**

A. they split up
B. they have a child
C. they get married
D. Bonnie passes away

Quiz 4 Answer Key

1. **(B)** 1947
2. **(A)** in childbirth
3. **(A)** Mr. Death
4. **(D)** his daughter
5. **(D)** "it felt right in my heart"
6. **(B)** his woman
7. **(D)** Rose
8. **(A)** his graduation
9. **(A)** a rag
10. **(C)** blues
11. **(D)** "you don't count here"
12. **(D)** Troy
13. **(B)** make him scared
14. **(A)** a baseball bat
15. **(B)** on the other side of the fence
16. **(D)** three
17. **(C)** eight
18. **(C)** 1986
19. **(B)** a chorus
20. **(A)** it has no mouthpiece
21. **(C)** the gates of heaven
22. **(B)** 1965
23. **(C)** the garden
24. **(C)** the Marines
25. **(A)** they split up

ClassicNotes

GradeSaver™

Getting you the grade since 1999™

Other ClassicNotes from GradeSaver™

Made in the USA
Lexington, KY
14 May 2012